AMAZING!

INTERVIEWS AND CONVERSATIONS

AMAZING!

Interviews and Conversations

WRITTEN AND ILLUSTRATED BY

SUSAN BATES

Vancouver Community College

Prentice Hall Canada Inc., Scarborough, Ontario

Canadian Cataloguing in Publication Data

Bates, Susan
Amazing! : interviews and conversations

Companion to: Amazing! : Canadian newspaper stories.
ISBN 0-13-012386-2

1. English language - Textbooks for second language learners.* 2. Readers (Adult). 3. Reading (Adult education) - Problems, exercises, etc.
4. Reading comprehension - Problems, exercises, etc.
I. Title.

PE1128.B38 1992 428.6'4 C92-094577-5

Prentice Hall, Inc., Englewood Cliffs, New Jersey
Prentice-Hall International, Inc., London
Prentice-Hall of Australia, Pty., Ltd., Sydney
Prentice-Hall of India Pvt., Ltd., New Delhi
Prentice-Hall of Japan, Inc., Tokyo
Prentice-Hall of Southeast Asia (Pte.) Ltd., Singapore
Editora Prentice-Hall do Brasil Ltda., Rio de Janeiro
Prentice-Hall Hispanoamericana, S.A., Mexico

ISBN 0-13-012386-2

Acquisitions Editor: Marjorie Walker
Developmental Editor: Linda Gorman
Copy Editor: Sheldon Fischer
Production Editor: Kelly Dickson
Production Coordinator: Florence Rousseau
Design: Monica Kompter
Page Layout: Laura Ball

1 2 3 4 5 AP 97 96 95 94 93

Printed and bound in Canada by Alger Press Limited

TABLE OF CONTENTS

PREFACE

TO THE INSTRUCTOR

Amazing! Interviews and Conversations is an innovative listening and speaking text designed to give high-beginner/low-intermediate ESL students a unique glimpse at Canadians and their culture. Themes explored include dating and marriage, pets, raising children, Canadian immigration, and opening your own business—just to name the first five!

Not only does this inventive new book contain authentic interviews with Canadians from Vancouver Island to Newfoundland, but the interview topics relate directly to the newspaper stories found in the original *Amazing! Canadian Newspaper Stories*. The books are in fact companion texts. Each one stands easily on its own, but the two are a set and work exceedingly well together.

To top it all off, there are two excellent new chapters, the newspaper stories are presented in a refreshing conversation or interview format, plus there's a separate section on functional language featuring a variety of stimulating listening and speaking activities.

RATIONALE

The concept of developing a companion text stems from Krashen's notion (1981) that second language acquisition is enhanced through the use of narrow input. In other words, students tend to retain more if lessons are based on specific topics or themes. The building of schematic knowledge in a particular area enables students not only to classify incoming information, but the added background leaves them freer to deal with progressively more complex linguistic and semantic data.

UNDERSTANDING LISTENING

Listening, like reading, is an interactive process in which the listener makes simultaneous use of a variety of strategies to process an incoming message. To a certain extent, she/he processes the words and phrases heard, but to a greater extent, she/he interprets the message by comparing it to the background knowledge she/he already possesses. Only then can the meaning of incoming information be truly integrated and understood.

The "Facts" section at the beginning of every chapter provides students with just the background knowledge they need to obtain a substantial grasp of the selected cultural topic. Pre-reading and discussion activities in the instructor's manual allow for a deeper understanding of this material and therefore a more adequate preparation for all of the listening and speaking activities which follow.

The Chapters

SECTION 1: CANADIAN CULTURE

As mentioned, each chapter begins with a list of cultural facts. These are gathered from the most recent Statistics Canada publications and are intended as a starting point for intercultural discussion.

The cultural theme is explored further in a "woman/man-on-the-street" interview. Students are highly motivated as they listen to authentic interviews with a cross-section of Canadians who offer their views on a series of open-ended questions. Through performing related listening tasks and participating in follow-up discussions, students gain insight into how Canadians think and feel. This is invaluable information for newcomers and visitors alike.

The section concludes with a speaking activity revolving around similar interview questions. Students are encouraged to share information about their countries in a classroom interaction or inquire further about Canadians in a contact assignment. These combined activities allow for intercultural enrichment and understanding, not to mention a widened schematic framework which enables them to comprehend the "Listening to the Story" section more fully.

SECTION 2: LISTENING TO THE STORY

This section is based upon an interview or conversation which relates the events of the newspaper story and corresponds to the sequence of nine illustrations. As in the first section, students listen to an extended dialogue so they may gain exposure to the natural flow of the language and "quantity listening experience" needed for optimal learning (Ur, 1983). Furthermore, the interaction of aural and visual cues along with previously activated background knowledge authenticates "real-life" listening in that students make simultaneous use of a variety of strategies to process the incoming message.

In "real-life" situations, we listen for one of two basic reasons: either we listen for general meaning or we listen for specific information. The task design in *Amazing!* reflects these authentic listening purposes. In this section for example, visual support incorporated into the initial exercise guides students to listen for gist so that they may retell the story afterwards. During subsequent listenings, students extract specific information. They listen and make short responses as the tape is being played.

After completing the pre-assigned tasks and the desired comprehension has been obtained, students are given an opportunity to react to the story. This activity, sometimes found in the instructor's manual, encourages students to make inferences about characters or events, discuss the story, or relate some aspect of it to their own personal experience.

SECTION 3: FUNCTIONAL CONVERSATIONS

The third and final section of each chapter is based on short conversations which relate to the newspaper story. These conversations focus on specific language functions or conversation management strategies relevant to the students' lives. Following each listening activity is a complementary speaking exercise. These vary from chapter to chapter and include communicative dyads, simulated role-plays and problem-solving tasks.

Outstanding Features

AUTHENTIC SPEECH

Current research in listening and speaking (Anderson and Lynch, 1987; Bygate, 1988) promotes the use of authentic speech even with students at a beginner level. If second language learners are ever going to understand native speakers in a natural context, it is imperative that they be exposed to authentic discourse complete with hesitations, false starts, self-corrections, rephrasings, and overlapping turns.

Ur (1983) believes this is not entirely the case. She feels that students at a low level of language competence could not even begin to understand unscripted dialogue, and as a classroom instructor with over fifteen years experience, I would have to agree. This, however, does not mean that in scripting dialogues for high beginners/low intermediates one should abandon all that current research has to offer. We now know how different spoken language is from its written counterpart. Along with the aforementioned characteristics, speech differs from writing in its redundancy, clausal nature of word groupings, and spontaneous discourse. The tapescript has been designed with careful attention to the characteristics of authentic speech. In fact, scripts for Section 1 are based on actual live recordings. Only minimal changes were necessary to make them comprehensible for the intended level.

CANADIAN CULTURE

A second outstanding feature of this text lies in its focus on Canadian culture. The federal government, in revising the curriculum mandate for ESL, has identified "the orientation to Canadian culture" as one of its primary objectives.

Amazing! Interviews and Conversations provides high beginners/low intermediates with an array of facinating cultural data promoting discussions about the country and fostering an attitude of tolerence and intercultural understanding.

Supplementary Materials

CASSETTE TAPES

The cassette tapes are an integral part of the entire package. They incorporate background noise, and authentic Canadian speakers with a variety of regional and international accents.

INSTRUCTOR'S MANUAL

The instructor's manual contains pre-reading and discussion activities for the "Facts" section, detailed suggestions for the listening and speaking activities in every chapter plus the complete tapescript, answer key, and supplementary materials such as card games, quizzes, and contact assignments.

PREFACE

TO THE STUDENT

Amazing! Interviews and Conversations is a great new listening and speaking book for English as a Second Language students. First and most important, this book will help you understand Canadian speakers more easily. The exercises will help you listen to real-life, natural language and understand it.

You'll learn all about Canadians and their culture. You'll find out about dating and marriage, pets, raising children, Canadian immigration, and opening your own business—and that's not all! There are fourteen chapters with up-to-date cultural facts and interviews with Canadians from across the country.

The fourteen cultural topics relate to the stories in another book you may already know—*Amazing! Canadian Newspaper Stories*. Both contain the same stories but in the listening book you'll learn about the newspaper story through an interview with someone from the story, or by listening to people talk about what happened.

The final section of every chapter includes short conversations. You'll learn different language functions like inviting, complimenting, thanking, comparing, making deals, asking politely, and many others. These conversations will help you do these same things in your day-to-day life.

Of course, you'll need the cassettes to go with the book so you can listen and complete all of the exercises. Answers are in the Instructor's Manual, so ask your teacher if you'd like to check them yourself. You may also want to read along as you listen. Again, ask your teacher. The tapescript is in the Instructor's Manual.

ACKNOWLEDGMENTS

First of all, I would like to thank Marjorie Walker, Acquisitions Editor at Prentice Hall Canada for her encouragement and guidance.

I also very much appreciated the thoughtful suggestions offered by Linda Gorman, Developmental Editor, Kelly Dickson, Production Editor, and Sheldon Fischer, Copy Editor also at Prentice Hall.

My thanks go to Pat Coleman of Coleman and Company Production Ltd. for his expertise in producing the cassettes.

I would like to thank my reviewers: Jas Gill, English Language Institute, UBC; Karen Hammond, Alberta Vocational College—Calgary; Nancy Phillips, Centennial College; Judith Roth, Vancouver School Board; and Carole Trepanier, UBC Language Institute, for their invaluable suggestions and commentary.

Thank you very much to the administration and faculty of Vancouver Community College, King Edward Campus, for their interest and support.

Especially, I would like to thank Fraser Thorburn for his thorough review and field testing of the final manuscript.

I am grateful to both Joan Cawsey and Fraser Thorburn for their input on the cassette production.

Special thanks to Chris Clark for her in-depth review on an earlier version of the text.

My genuine appreciation goes to John Kostoff, Mike Webb, Fraser Thorburn and Lee Aceman for their help in recording an earlier version of the tapescript.

Thank you also to the many instructors from the Vocational, Outreach, and ELS Departments of King Edward Campus, Vancouver Community College, who field tested and provided feedback for Section 2 of the book.

Special mention goes to Dr. Rolland Lewis at UBC for sharing research from his most recent thesis dealing with ESL and sources of funding.

And finally, a big thank you to Robert McDonald and Eve Mendez for listening to me and offering advice on both *Amazing! Canadian Newspaper Stories* and *Amazing! Interviews and Conversations.*

CHAPTER 1: DATING AND MARRIAGE

Derek Brenchley and Marcela Sanchez, Courtenay, B.C.

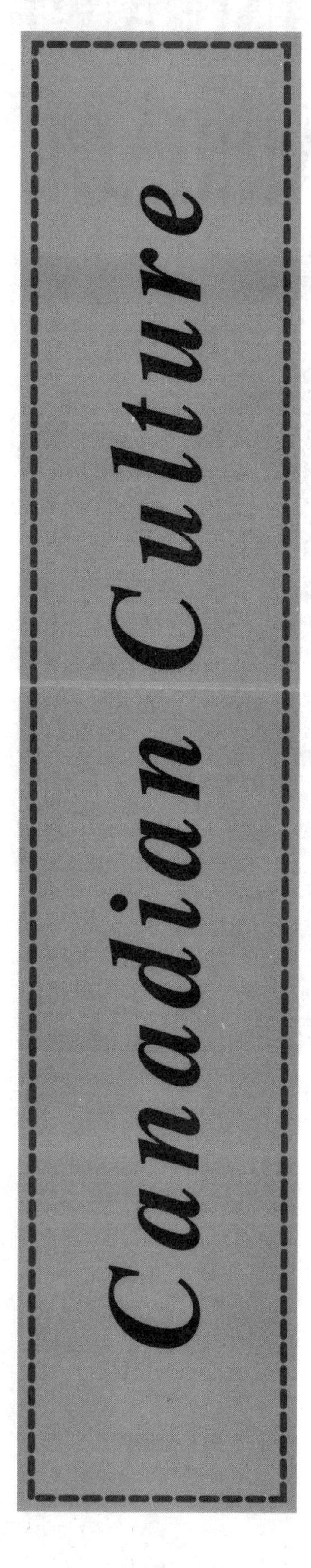

DATING AND MARRIAGE

FACTS:

1. Most Canadians begin dating in their early teenage years.

2. Young people often go out in groups and meet at school dances or house parties.

3. After dating a number of different partners, many teenagers begin "going out with" or "seeing" one special person at about 16 or 17 years of age.

4. Eighty-seven percent of 15 - 19 year olds think sex before marriage is fine if the two people love each other.

5. The three most popular first dates for those over 20 are lunch, dinner, or a movie.

6. People are staying single longer than they did 10 or 20 years ago.

7. First-time brides are usually around 26 years old. Grooms are about 28.

8. Thirty-eight percent of men and 30% of women aged 20 - 24 live together.

9. Sixty-three percent of all common-law relationships end in marriage.

10. Today, fewer people are getting married, and fewer divorced people are getting remarried.

11. A higher percentage of Canadians are staying single or living together.

12. Eighty-five percent of Canadians get married.

**Instructor's Manual:* Pre-reading activity and discussion
Alternate Activity: Have students relate these cultural facts to information about dating and marriage in their countries.

LISTENING TO CANADIANS — Interview 1

Before You Listen: 1. Talk about the meaning of these words:

fellow (fella) | body language | in common | Easter

2. Read the statements below. Ask about any words you don't know.

Listen and tick off [✔] all correct statements. Mark an "x" beside those that are wrong. Correct the mistakes.

1. ☐ Derek is 24 years old.
2. ☐ He lives in Courtenay on Vancouver Island in BC.
3. ☐ He has been married fourteen and a half years.
4. ☐ Derek met his wife in the Dominican Republic.
5. ☐ He went there to work for ten years.
6. ☐ He met Marcela at a disco.
7. ☐ Marcela was a pre-school teacher and Derek was a police officer.

Derek Brenchley and Marcela Sanchez, Courtenay, B.C.

8. ☐ He liked her because of the physical attraction.
9. ☐ She wasn't very much fun but there was a lot of life in her eyes.
10. ☐ They went out dancing the first time they met.
11. ☐ Marcela showed Derek around the country and taught him to speak Dominican.
12. ☐ They went out for five years before they got married.
13. ☐ They lived together for ten years because they felt it was important to get to know each other before marriage.
14. ☐ They got engaged on Valentine's Day, February the 14th.
15. ☐ Derek gave Marcela a card and written on it was "Yo te amo" which means "I love you" in Spanish.
16. ☐ They got married six weeks later on Christmas day. Derek proposed when he gave Marcela the charm, the bracelet, and the pendant, or necklace.

**Instructor's Manual*
Tapescript and discussion

LISTENING TO CANADIANS — Interviews 2 & 3

Before You Listen: Talk about the meaning of these words:

mature	garage	golden wedding	anniversary
good-hearted	outgoing	eloped	scared

Listen to the second two interviews as many times as you need to fill in the missing information about Donna and Lillian.

Name: From: Age: Years Married:	Donna Taylor Toronto, Ont. 32 years old 11 years	Lillian & Albert Hareuther Edmonton, Alta. 75 years old 49 years
1. How did you meet your husband/wife?		
2. What did you like about him/her?		
3. How long did you go out before you got married?		
4. Did you live together?		
5. Did you get engaged? For how long?		
6. Who proposed? How?		

**Instructor's Manual*
Tapescript and discussion

SPEAKING — MARRIED PEOPLE

Interview Talk to two married people. Write short answers.

Name: Years Married:		
1. How old were you on your first date?		
2. How many people did you go out with before you met your husband/wife?		
3. How did you meet your husband/wife?		
4. What did you like about him/her?		
5. How long did you go out before you got married?		
6. Did you live together? For how long?		
7. Did you get engaged? For how long?		
8. Who proposed? How?		
9. What kind of wedding did you have?		
10. Did you go on a honeymoon? Tell about it.		

In what unusual ways could someone propose marriage?

Listening to the Story

WHEAT FARMER SURPRISES GIRLFRIEND

First Listening: A woman is telling her husband about a newspaper story she read. Listen and follow the pictures.

Tell the story.

Read it in *Amazing! Canadian Newspaper Stories.*
Tapescript in *Instructor's Manual*

Listening to the Story—Wheat Farmer Surprises Girlfriend

LISTENING FOR FACTS

Second Listening: You are a newspaper reporter. Listen to the conversation and write the facts in the chart.

Who: 1. *Chuck, the farmer* 2. ________________	**Where:** 1. ____________ 2. *Regina*
Why: *He* ____________ *Cecile and wanted to* ____________ *her.*	**How:** *He got on his* ____________ ...
When: *. . . at* ____________ *in the morning.*	**What:** *He cut a* ____________ *in his* ____________ ____________.
How long: (time) ____________ *hours and* ____________ *minutes* (kilometres) ____________ *km*	**What happened:** *He rented a* ____________ *and flew Cecile over the* ________. *She said, "* ____________ *!"*

Reacting to the Story—Wheat Farmer Surprises Girlfriend

SPEAKING — VIDEO PRESS CONFERENCE

Writing: You are a newspaper reporter. Write down questions for Chuck and Cecile.

Questions for Chuck

____?

____?

Questions for Cecile

____?

____?

SPEAKING

Role Play: Work in groups of three. One person is a newspaper reporter and asks questions to Chuck and Cecile.

Press Conference: Work with the class. Two people play the parts of Chuck and Cecile—they sit at the front of the class. All other students are reporters and go up one at a time to ask their question(s). Videotape the conference.

WHAT'S IMPORTANT IN A MATE?

With a Partner Here are some qualities you may find important in a mate. What is the meaning of each quality? Put the number of the meaning beside the correct quality.

hard working _____	1. smart
mature _____	2. likes to help
generous _____	3. happy all the time
helpful _____	4. doesn't have other boy/girlfriends
neat _____	5. makes you laugh
outgoing _____	6. has lots of money
dependable _____	7. good looking
faithful _____	8. doesn't lie, tells the truth
intelligent _____	9. understands your problems
rich _____	10. gives, shares
attractive _____	11. not messy
funny _____	12. acts like an adult, not a child
honest _____	13. friendly, active
cheerful _____	14. works a lot
considerate _____	15. you can trust this person
understanding _____	16. thinks of other people's feelings

With a Group Cut these out* and put them in order starting with the quality everyone thinks is most important for a mate.

hard working	mature	generous	helpful
neat	outgoing	dependable	faithful
intelligent	rich	attractive	funny
honest	cheerful	considerate	understanding

CULTURE NOTE: What do Canadians want in a mate? See last page of chapter for answer.

**Instructor's Manual*
Adjective card masters

INVITING

First Listening: Listen to each conversation and tick off [✔] the answers to the following questions.

CONVERSATION 1

Who's inviting?

Chuck ☐

Cecile ☐

What's the invitation?

dancing ☐

dinner ☐

Other person answers...

yes ☐

no ☐

CONVERSATION 2

Who's inviting?

Chuck ☐

Cecile ☐

What's the invitation?

meet parents ☐

meet children ☐

Other person answers...

yes ☐

no ☐

CONVERSATION 3

Who's inviting?

Chuck ☐

Cecile ☐

What's the invitation?

go to Bob's birthday party ☐

go to Mary's birthday party ☐

Other person says...

yes ☐

no ☐

CONVERSATION 4

Who's inviting?

Chuck ☐

Cecile ☐

What's the invitation?

go to a movie ☐

clean up the apartment ☐

Other person says...

yes ☐

no ☐

EXTRA

1. What is the second invitation in conversation 4? ______________________
2. Who does the inviting? ______________________
3. What is unusual about the invitation? ______________________
4. What does the other person say? ______________________

WHAT DO THEY SAY?

Second Listening: Write the number of the conversation beside each question or answer.

SETTING UP AN INVITATION

☐ Are you busy this Saturday?

☐ How's everything going?

☐ Mary called. She's planning a surprise party for Bob.

☐ What'cha doing? (What are you doing?)

☐ Mom was talking about having you over for dinner.

____

____

INVITING

☐ (Do) You want to go?

☐ How about coming over (and cleaning up my place)?

☐ What do you say we go out for dinner?

☐ What do you think?

____

____

ACCEPTING—SAYING YES

☐ Sounds good to me.

☐ Sure.

☐ I'd love to.

☐ I'd like that.

____

____

REFUSING—SAYING NO

☐ We're busy.

☐ We have other plans.

☐ I'd really like to, but...(I have to wash my hair)

☐ Maybe some other time.

____

____

Think of two different ways to set up an invitation, to invite, to accept, and to refuse. Write them in the spaces above.

SPEAKING WITH A PARTNER

First read the tapescripts, and then use this page and the one just before it to help you practice the conversations without the script.

**Instructor's Manual*
Tapescript

SPEAKING — MAKE A DATE!

Partner 1: This is an appointment book for two days. Find out when your partner is free and then invite him/her 1) to go for a walk, and 2) to go cycling. Use the expressions from the last page.

DON'T LOOK AT YOUR PARTNER'S APPOINTMENT BOOK!

Monday		Tuesday	
10:00	*Swimming with Sarah*	10:00	
12:00		12:00	*Lunch with Steve*
2:00		2:00	
4:00		4:00	
6:00	*English class*	6:00	
8:00	*English class*	8:00	

Partner 2: This is your appointment book for two days. Say yes or no to your partner's invitations and then invite him/her 1) to meet you for coffee, and 2) to go to a movie. Use the expressions from the last page.

DON'T LOOK AT YOUR PARTNER'S APPOINTMENT BOOK!

Monday		Tuesday	
10:00		10:00	
12:00	*Immigration appointment*	12:00	
2:00		2:00	
4:00	*Shopping with Peter*	4:00	*Marriage prep. course*
6:00		6:00	
8:00		8:00	

CULTURE NOTE: What do Canadians want in a mate? They want someone who is dependable, honest, faithful, considerate, understanding, cheerful, and mature.

CHAPTER 2: PETS

Bonnie Enns, Vancouver, B.C.

Mike Dionne, Sarnia, Ont.

Canadian Culture

PETS

FACTS:

1. Forty-two percent of Canadians have pets. There are over 5 000 000 pets in the country.

2. There are 2 205 000 dogs, 2 044 000 cats and 1 093 000 other pets like birds, rabbits, hamsters, gerbils, mice, snakes and fish.

3. People in the Atlantic provinces have the most pets. People in Quebec have the fewest.

4. Families spend about $316 a year on their pets, but some people spend a lot more; there are pet psychologists for "crazy" pets, beauty salons for rich pets, vets for sick pets and cemeteries for dead pets. It costs $200 to bury a cat and $300 to bury a dog at one cemetery in Ontario.

5. Doctors say that pets help people relax. When people talk to other people, their blood pressure usually goes up, but when they talk to a pet it usually goes down. This means they feel comfortable and relaxed.

6. Blood pressure goes down even when people look at a tank of goldfish.

7. Doctors studied some people who had heart attacks. They found out that if the person had a pet, they were twice as likely to get better.

8. Doctors also say that if you have a pet, it's easier to make friends. People walking outside with their pets have more conversations with others and also have longer conversations.

9. Many families have fewer arguments and spend more time playing together after they get a pet.

**Instructor's Manual*
Pre-reading activity and discussion
Alternate Activity: Have students make up a question about each fact and then ask them of a partner.

LISTENING TO CANADIANS — Interview 1

Before You Listen: 1. Talk about the meaning of these words:

thump	ended up	seeds
vet	humans	messy

2. Read the statements below. Ask about any words you don't know.

Listen and tick off [✓] all correct statements. Mark an "x" beside those that are wrong. Correct the mistakes.

1. ☐ Bonnie has a special kind of parrot, a cockatoo.
2. ☐ Her pet's name is Thumper.
3. ☐ She's had him for eighteen years.
4. ☐ She took the parrot when she stopped living with her boyfriend.
5. ☐ She takes care of him by talking to him, playing with him, and taking him outside.
6. ☐ She feeds him ice cream.
7. ☐ He cleans his own cage.
8. ☐ She takes him outside every day if she can. He always goes out with her on the weekend.
9. ☐ Sometimes, she takes him in the shower with her and then she gives him a blow dry with her hair dryer.
10. ☐ She likes him because he is friendly, funny and very affectionate.
11. ☐ He talks, he meows like a cat and barks like a dog.
12. ☐ He makes a noise like a cow and does a little dance.
13. ☐ He says, "Hi, hello, I'm Thumper," and "I'm not feeling very well today," and "Bye-bye."
14. ☐ At home he talks more. He says, "Bye-bye, go for a walk. See you later," "I love you," and "Handsome bird."

Bonnie Enns, Vancouver, B.C.

**Instructor's Manual*
Tapescript and discussion

LISTENING TO CANADIANS — Interviews 2 & 3

Before You Listen: 1. Talk about the meaning of these words:

I'm serious!	scratch	boa python	aquarium	gerbils
hamsters	wraps around	poisonous	bite	well-fed

2. What questions will the interviewer ask?

Listen to the second two interviews as many times as you need to fill in the missing information.

Crystal Singer's pet, Regina, Saskatchewan

1. Kind: ______________________
2. Name: ______________________
3. Age: ______________________
4. Why got: ______________________
____
____
5. How to care for: ______________________
____
____
____
6. What owner likes: ______________________
____
____
7. Anything unusual: ______________________
____
____
____

Mike Dionne and his pet, Sarnia, Ontario

1. Kind: ______________________
2. Name: ______________________
3. Age: ______________________
4. Why got: ______________________
____
____
5. How to care for: ______________________
____
____
____
6. What owner likes: ______________________
____
____
7. Anything unusual: ______________________
____
____
8. How many: ______________________

SPEAKING — BLACKBOARD STORIES

IN SMALL GROUPS

Interview a student who has had a pet. First work together to make up questions. (You may want to use some of those from the taped interview.) Then ask the questions, take notes, and use your notes to write a story on the blackboard. Correct these stories with the class.

QUESTIONS

1. ______________________________?
2. ______________________________?
3. ______________________________?
4. ______________________________?
5. ______________________________?
6. ______________________________?
7. ______________________________?

CLASS DISCUSSION

1. Is it usual or normal for people to have pets in your country? If so, what kinds of pets do they have? Why do they have pets?
2. In Canada, people often eat beef, but the cow is thought of as a sacred animal in India so people there do not eat beef. Are there any animals people think are special in your country?
3. In some countries, people eat monkey brains, snakes, and even cats and dogs. Do you think this is any different from eating fish, chickens, or cows? Why or why not?
4. How can pets or animals help people? Do you know of animals that work or do some special job for people?
5. How can pets help people with disabilities? What kinds of pets can help them?
6. Do you think animals are intelligent? Why or why not?

DEBBIE'S DOG

First Listening: Debbie is being interviewed on a radio talk show. Listen to the interview and follow the pictures.

What is funny about the pictures? Are they 100% correct? Tell the story.

*Read it in *Amazing! Canadian Newspaper Stories.*

Listening to the Story

HOW DOES HE DO IT?

Listen again and fill in the chart with information about how Gia, the dog, does each of the following things.

1. He answers the phone:
2. He gets things Debbie wants off the shelves:
3. He puts things in the shopping cart:
4. He pays the cashier:
5. He understands things:

Functional Conversations

COMPLIMENTING

First Listening: Listen to four conversations. Mark a "g" beside the person who gives the compliment and an "a" beside the person who accepts it.

CONVERSATION 1

_____ man ____ Debbie

CONVERSATION 2

_____ Debbie ____ Cashier

CONVERSATION 3

_____ Debbie ____ Mr. Parks

CONVERSATION 4

_____ Brenda ____ Mr. Parks

COMPLIMENTING

Second Listening: Write the number of the conversation beside each of the expressions for giving and accepting compliments.

GIVING

☐ You're looking very **nice** today! (handsome/well-dressed)

☐ Great **haircut!** (watch/ring/sweater)

☐ **He's** really a **friendly dog!** (She/ happy child)

☐ What a helpful **dog** you have! (neighbour)

☐ **He's** so **quiet** and **well-behaved.** (She/intelligent/outgoing)

☐ That's a real **smart dog!** (lovely pair of earings)

☐ It looks very **professional.** (expensive/becoming/elegant)

☐ **He** looks so **strong** and **healthy**. (It/ well-made/durable)

☐ You're doing a **good** job. (great/fantastic/excellent)

____

____

I (like/love) your (TV/car/boyfriend)!
You've got a (lovely/beautiful) (apartment/new sofa).

ACCEPTING

☐ Glad you like **it**. (him/them)

☐ Thanks for the compliment.

☐ I'm glad you like **him**. (it/them)

☐ That's nice of you to say.

☐ I think so too.

☐ Why, thank you.

☐ That's nice to (know/hear).

Practice other compliments by substituting the words in brackets for those in bold print. Next think of other ways of giving and accepting compliments and write them on the spaces above.

SPEAKING — COMPLIMENTARY CIRCLES

With the Class Stand in two circles—one inside the other. Make sure there is the same number of students in the inner and outer circles. Students in the inside begin by complimenting the person standing in front of them on everything from clothing to haircuts to jewellery to their English. Then, the insiders all move to the right and students in the outer circle take turns complimenting insiders. This continues until the circle has turned once around.

CHAPTER 3: RAISING CHILDREN

Eric Minhas and Roop Sandhu

Canadian Culture

CHILDREN AND FAMILIES

FACTS:

1. There are 5.6 million Canadian girls and boys under 15 years of age.
2. Canada's children have different ethnic backgrounds. Forty-three percent have origins other than British or French.
3. Eighty-five percent of children live with both parents. Eleven percent live with their mothers and 2% with their fathers.
4. Sixty-four percent of children live in families with both parents working.
5. Both parents work full-time in 29% of families.
6. Fifty-seven percent of married women with children under six are working. Educated women are most likely to have jobs.
7. Seventy-one percent of children live in single, detached homes. Fourteen percent live in doubles, row-houses or duplexes. Thirteen percent live in apartments.
8. Ninety-eight percent of homes have a colour TV. Children watch less TV than adults. Those aged 2 - 11 watch close to 20 hours a week while adults watch around 24.
9. Across Canada, there are about 7 000 day care centres and 298 000 spaces for children. This is enough for only 14% of all children who need day care.
10. The usual family size is smaller now (3.1 people) than it was 10 years ago (3.7 people). This is because people are having fewer children and more families have only a single parent.
11. Seventy-three percent of Canadians think discipline in the home is not strict enough. Two percent say it's too strict and 19% think it's just about right.
12. Most people say that family is the most important part of their lives.

**Instructor's Manual*

True/false quiz and discussion

Alternate activity: Discuss how these facts compare with information about children and families in your students' countries.

LISTENING TO CANADIANS — Interview 1

Before You Listen: Discuss the meaning of these words:

grow up I could go on forever. stitches awful

Listen and write short answers.

Name: From: Age:	Victor Bennett Ottawa, Ontario 44 years old
1. How many children do you have?	
2. What are their ages?	
3. What are some of the good things about having children?	
4. What are some of the problems?	
5. Can you tell about a time when one of your children was in danger or had an accident?	
6. Would you like to have more children?	

**Instructor's Manual*
Tapescript and discussion

LISTENING TO CANADIANS — DISCIPLINE

Read the statements below and say if you agree or disagree.

Listen to the second speaker, Anne Marie Dibbs, to find out what she has to say about discipline. Listen until the interviewer says, "You taught them right from wrong."

Tick off [✔] each of the statements she makes.

1. ☐ I hit them whenever they needed it.
2. ☐ I brought them up Christian.
3. ☐ I taught them to be honest, to tell the truth.
4. ☐ I always told the teachers and the principal right in front of my children to discipline them if they needed it.
5. ☐ I would ground them.
6. ☐ Oh, when they were small, a few times I had to spank them too, but they learn fast.
7. ☐ Parents have children and they do not take enough time to see what they're doing or care about what their children are are up to.
8. ☐ When the kids are small, you have to teach them not to hit other children.
9. ☐ I think parents should find out what their children are doing, where they are going.
10. ☐ There would be a lot less crime and a lot less trouble with the children if you talk to your children, listen to your children and care for them.
11. ☐ They know what is ours and if it's somebody else's, leave it alone—leave it where they find it instead of taking it.

Anne Marie Dibbs, Whitehorse, Yukon.

CLASS DISCUSSION

1. How do parents discipline children in your country?
2. Do you think Canadian parents are stricter or more lenient than parents in your country? Why do you think so?
3. Do you think it is right to hit or spank a child?
4. What are some things parents can do to help raise a happy child?/an unhappy child?
5. Do you think working mothers and fathers spend enough time with their children?

LISTENING TO CANADIANS — Interview 2

Before You Listen: Discuss the meaning of these words:

grown up	keep company	Christian	discipline
spank	ground	crime	toboggan
bruises	broken bones	guardian angel	miracle

Listen and write short answers.

Name: From: Age:	Anne Marie Dibbs Whitehorse, Yukon 50 years old
1. How many children do you have?	
2. What are their ages?	
3. What are some of the good things about having children?	
4. What are some of the problems?	
5. Can you tell about a time when one of your children was in danger or had an accident?	
6. Would you like to have more children?	

LISTENING TO CANADIANS — Interview 3

Before You Listen: Discuss the meaning of these words:

emotional things	I suppose	well-behaved
exercise bicycle	bare feet	broke the bone

Listen and write short answers.

Name: From: Age:	Sheila Adair Kerr Mississauga, Ont. 36 years old
1. How many children do you have?	
2. What are their ages?	
3. What are some of the good things about having children?	
4. What are some of the problems?	
5. Can you tell about a time when one of your children was in danger or had an accident?	
6. Would you like to have more children?	

**Instructors Manual*
Tapescript and discussion

ROOP SAVES THE DAY

First Listening: A newspaper reporter finds Mrs. Minhas, Eric's mother, in a hospital waiting room shortly after Eric's fall. Listen to their conversation and put the pictures in order.

Tell the story.

*Read it in *Amazing! Canadian Newspaper Stories.* Tapescript in *Instructor's Manual.*

CORRECT THE REPORTER'S NOTES

Second Listening: Correct the reporter's notes. Mark an "x" beside anything that is wrong. Then listen again to correct the mistakes.

1. ☐ *Mrs. M was working when Eric fell*

2. ☐ *she and Eric fell asleep*

3. ☐ *Eric carried the sofa onto balcony*

4. ☐ *kids were playing on balcony*

5. ☐ *Eric saw them*

6. ☐ *he went onto balcony*

7. ☐ *he got on the chair*

8. ☐ *he fell off the chair*

9. ☐ *he slipped on the edge of the balcony*

10. ☐ *he held onto edge*

11. ☐ *he screamed for help*

12. ☐ *husband was watching TV*

13. ☐ *Eric started falling*

14. ☐ *he fell sixteen storeys*

15. ☐ *Roop was playing with children*

16. ☐ *he threw out the garbage*

17. ☐ *he started walking, arms out*

18. ☐ *he caught Eric*

19. ☐ *Eric is going to be all right*

THANKING

Listen to the following conversations and write the number of the conversation beside the expressions for thanking and accepting thanks.

THANKING (formal to informal)	**ACCEPTING THANKS**
____ We would like to take this to opportunity thank...	____ We're glad to help out.
____ We are here today to express our appreciation to...	____ Thank you.
____ We hope this medal will help you remember how grateful we are.	____ Glad to be of help, really.
____ I really appreciate you...	____ Don't mention it.
____ My husband and I are extremely grateful.	____ Oh, it's nothing, really.
____ We really didn't know how to thank you.	____ My pleasure.
____ I'm not sure I really know how to thank you.	____ No problem.
____ I never really got the chance to thank you.	
____ Thank you again.	
____ That was really thoughtful.	
____ Thanks a lot.	
____ Thanks a lot, sweetheart.	
____ This is great, honey!	
____ You didn't have to do that.	

SPEAKING

Practice the following situations with a partner. Which ones are formal and which are informal?

Thank your teacher for a great class at the "last day" party.	Thank your mother for taking care of your children.
Thank your neighbour for taking care of your house while you were away for a few days.	Thank a lady on the street for saving your life by pulling you away from an oncoming car.
Thank your boss for giving you a raise.	Thank your husband/wife for marrying you!

CHAPTER 4: IMMIGRATION

If you want to do something here, you can!
Margaretha Nordine, Saltspring Island, B.C.

FACTS:

1. Canada is a land of immigrants. Many scholars think that even the native people came here from Asia many thousands of years ago.

2. Immigration is important in maintaining the Canadian population or keeping about the same number of people in the country. This is because Canadians are having fewer and fewer children. If immigration does not go up, soon we will have fewer people living in Canada.

3. Sixteen percent of the population or more than 4 000 000 people were not born in this country.

4. Immigrants today come from the following countries:
   50% from Asia
   26% from Europe
   13% from the Caribbean, Central and South America
   7% from Africa
   3% from the U.S.
   1% from Oceania.

5. Immigrants come into Canada under three different classes: family, independent, and refugee. Around 45% of applicants are independent, 35% are family class, and 20% are refugees.

6. Most applicants are young. Eighty percent are under 40. Fifty-six percent are under 30.

7. Most immigrants settle in Ontario, Quebec, B.C., and Alberta.

8. Most settle in large cities:
   34% go to Toronto
   14% go to Montreal
   10% go to Vancouver
   5% go to Calgary
   5% go to Edmonton.

9. Forty to fifty percent of newcomers cannot speak English or French when they arrive. After five years, 82% can speak one of Canada's two official languages. After 8.5 years, 92% have learned either English or French.

10. More immigrants are university graduates than non-immigrants. At the same time, more immigrants have less than a Grade 9 education than those born in Canada. In other words, immigrants usually have either a very high, or a very low, level of education.

11. Immigrants usually make higher yearly incomes than Canadian-born workers.

12. There are more independent applicants who are entrepreneurs, or investors: they are bringing jobs and money into the country. For example, last year B.C. welcomed 809 entrepreneurial immigrants with $1.2 billion and plans to create 3738 jobs for Canadians.

**Instructor's Manual*
True/false quiz

LISTENING TO CANADIANS — Interview 1

Before You Listen: Discuss the meaning of these words:

uncertain future	basically	multiculturalism	fit in
Chinese community	foreign	Boxing Day	scenery

Listen to the first speaker and complete his form for the immigration department.

IMMIGRATION REPORT	
Michael Mak, 42 years old	
1. Native country	2. Date arrived in Canada
3. Reason for leaving native country	
4. How applied	
5. Sponsor	6. Pay
7. Status/class	8. Wait for papers
9. Thoughts about Canada	
10. Biggest difference between Canada and native country	
11. First day in Canada	
12. First week in Canada	
13. Canada: a good country for immigrants?	
14. Plans for the future	

**Instructor's Manual*
Tapescript and discussion

LISTENING TO CANADIANS — Interview 2

Before You Listen: Discuss the meaning of these words.

Canadian Embassy	plane fare	opportunities	bilingualism
Chevrolet	highway	freeway	sticks in your mind

Listen to the second speaker and complete her form for the immigration department.

IMMIGRATION REPORT	
Margaretha Nordine, 50 years old	
1. Native country	2. Arrived in Canada
3. Why left native country	
4. How applied	
5. Sponsor	6. Pay
7. Status/class	8. Wait for papers
9. Thoughts about Canada	
10. Biggest difference between Canada and native country	
11. First day in Canada	
12. First week in Canada	
13. Canada: a good country for immigrants?	
14. Plans for the future	

**Instructor's Manual*
Tapescript and discussion

SPEAKING — IMMIGRATING TO CANADA

INTERVIEW

What questions did the interviewer ask Michael and Margaretha? Write them below and then ask them to a landed immigrant.

1. ____?
2. ____?
3. ____?
4. ____?
5. ____?
6. ____?
7. ____?
8. ____?
9. ____?
10. ____?
11. ____?
12. ____?
13. ____?
14. ____?

LOVERS UNITED

First Listening: A woman tells her husband about a newspaper story she read. Listen to the conversation and put the pictures in order.

Tell the story.

* Read it in *Amazing! Canadian Newspaper Stories.* Tapescript in *Instructor's Manual*

TRAVELLING

Second Listening: Listen again and fill in the chart showing Olga's and Vladimir's travels.

OLGA'S AND VLADIMIR'S TRAVELS				
When	Who	From	To	Why
1.				
2.				
3.				
4.				
5.				
6.				

CLASS DISCUSSION

1. Do you think Olga and Vladimir will stay married? Why or why not?
2. Do you think they were too old to get married? Why or why not?
3. What is the best age to get married?
4. In Canada, one in three marriages ends in divorce. Is divorce common or usual in your country? Why or why not?
5. What do you think of a man who marries three different women?
6. Do you think we should be able to have more than one husband or wife at the same time? Why or why not?

COMPARING

First Listening: Olga and Vladimir have three conversations. Write down what they are comparing in each of these conversations.

Conversation 1: ____________________

Conversation 2: ____________________

Conversation 3: ____________________

Second Listening: Listen again and write the number of the conversation beside each expression for comparing.

More

- ☐ far more (expensive)
- ☐ much more (handsome)
- ☐ a lot (greyer)
- ☐ definitely more (convenient)
- ☐ quite a bit more (heavy work)
- ☐ considerably (quieter)
- ☐ just a little (chubbier
- ☐ (pays) slightly more

Same

- ☐ (handsome) just the same
- ☐ as (beautiful)
- ☐ (Do you love me) just as much?

Less

- ☐ a lot less (traffic)

Verbs

- ☐ I prefer (living in a house)
- ☐ (Where) would you rather live?

Work with a group to see if you can think of other expressions for comparing. Write these in the spaces above.

SPEAKING — TWO-MINUTE CONVERSATIONS

With a Partner Compare the following items using "expressions for comparing" from the last exercise.

1. living in my country and living in Canada
2. getting married and living together
3. travelling by plane and travelling by train
4. writing a letter and calling long distance
5. riding a bicycle and driving a car
6. renting an apartment and buying a house
7. going to school and working full time
8. working part time and working full time
9. summer and winter
10. men and women

SPEAKING — ONE-MINUTE MONOLOGUES

With the Class Cut these out* and put them in a hat. One student picks one and has to compare the two items in front of the class.

watching TV swimming	chocolate vegetables	being a dancer being a social worker
doing the dishes cooking dinner	reading a book watching a movie	being single being married
my country Canada	driving walking	working nights working days
dog cat	being alone being with people	late for a party early for a party

**Instructor's Manual*
Comparison game card masters

CHAPTER 5: SMALL BUSINESS

Stephanie Yu, Vancouver, B.C.

Rui Amaral, Montreal, Que.

SMALL BUSINESS IN CANADA

FACTS:

1. There are more than 1.6 million self-employed people in Canada.

2. Half of these people work alone. The other half are employers: they pay additional workers.

3. The self-employed are people who own and operate a business, farm or professional practice (lawyers, accountants, engineers) as well as artists, writers, independent salespersons, fishermen, babysitters and newspaper carriers.

4. Seventeen percent of men and eight percent of women are self-employed.

5. A self-employed person is more likely to be married than a paid worker.

6. A self-employed worker is more likely to have a university degree, but many employers only have an elementary school education.

7. Older people are more likely to be self-employed:

age		
age	15-24	5%
	25-44	13%
	45-64	20%
	65+	46%

8. The average age for self-employed workers is 41.

9. More immigrants than non-immigrants are self-employed.

10. Self-employed workers work longer than paid workers. The self-employed usually work 46 hours a week whereas paid workers work only 36 hours.

**Instructor's Manual:* Pre-reading activity and discussion
Alternate Activity: Have students make up questions about each fact and ask them of a partner. Encourage "Why do you think . . . ?" questions.

LISTENING TO CANADIANS — Interview 1

Before You Listen: 1. Discuss the meaning of these words:

purchase | savings | look into it | wages

2. Read the statements below. Ask about any words you don't know.

Listen and tick off [✓] the statements that are correct. Mark an "x" beside those that are wrong. Correct the mistakes.

1. ☐ Stephanie has a dry-cleaning business.
2. ☐ It is called Stephanie's Dry Cleaning.
3. ☐ She opened it in 1977.
4. ☐ She bought the business from a good friend.
5. ☐ Stephanie borrowed from the bank.
6. ☐ Mrs. Yu learned the business through experience.
7. ☐ She didn't know anything about the business but she never made any mistakes.
8. ☐ Stephanie didn't like working for someone else.
9. ☐ She worked in a gas station before.
10. ☐ When you are working for someone else, you work longer hours and more days.
11. ☐ If you have your own business, there's less pressure 'cause you don't have a boss and you have more freedom.
12. ☐ If you work for someone else, you get a paycheque.
13. ☐ If you have your own business, you have to make sure the bills get paid and you have to write the paycheques.
14. ☐ Mrs. Yu works sixteen hours a week.
15. ☐ She wants to sell the business soon.
16. ☐ Having your own business is very challenging and if it's a success, it makes you feel good.

Stephanie Yu, 37, Vancouver, B.C.

**Instructor's Manual*
Tapescript and discussion

Listening to Canadians — Interview 2

Before You Listen: Discuss the meaning of these words:

night club	share (noun)	gross	profit
staff	expenses	disc jockey	well off

Listen to the interview as many times as you need to fill in the missing information.

1. Kind of business: ______________________
2. Name: ______________________
3. Where: ______________________
   ____
4. When: ______________________
   ____
   ____
   ____
5. Why: ______________________
   ____
   ____
   ____
   ____
   ____

Rui Amaral, 24, Montreal, Que.

6. What kind of music: ______________________
7. Band: ______________________
8. Best nights: ______________________
9. Cover charge: ______________________
10. Pros and cons: ______________________
    ____
    ____
    ____
    ____

Instructor's Manual
Tapescript and discussion

SPEAKING — BUSINESS PARTNERS

In Small Groups Talk about a business you would like to open and prepare a business presentation for the class. First discuss the questions below. Then make a chart to show important information on the blackboard.

1. What kind of business would you like to open?
2. How is it going to be better than what is now available?
   (Why will it be successful?)
3. What will you call it?
4. Where will you open it?
5. How will you start it?
6. How much money will you need? Where will you get it?
7. How many people will you hire?
8. How much will you charge?
9. What kind of special deals will you have on opening day?
10. What do you think your net profits will be per week/month/year?

(3) NAME OF BUSINESS
(1) TYPE OF BUSINESS:
(2) SPECIAL FEATURES:
(4) LOCATION:
(5-8) BUSINESS PLAN:
(9) OPENING DAY SPECIALS:
(10) PROFITS:

Sample chart for business presentation

MR. FIX-IT

First Listening: Two neighbours are talking outside their apartment building. Listen to their conversation and follow the pictures.

Tell the story.

*Read it in *Amazing! Canadian Newspaper Stories.* Tapescript in *Instructor's Manual*

NOEL'S PRICE LIST

First Listening: Listen and fill in the missing prices on Noel's price list.

NOEL'S PRICE LIST		
	REGULAR PRICE	SPECIAL DEAL
OUTDOOR WORK		
mow lawn	________	________
garden (3x4m)	75.00	________
(4x6m)	100.00	75.00
PLUMBING		
toilet —small problem	________	
—big problem	________	
leaking pipe	40.00	
broken pipe	80.00	
PLASTERING		
small hole/crack	________	
large hole/crack	________	
CARPENTRY		
small sundeck	________	
large sundeck	________	
ELECTRICAL WORK		
outdoor lighting	155.00	________
room	________	
house	600.00	________
MINIMUM $50.00 A VISIT		
25% OFF FOR SENIOR CITIZENS		

SPEAKING — CALLING FOR PRICES

Check your yellow pages under plumbing, plastering, gardening, carpentry, and electrical work. Find out prices for the items listed above.

NEGOTIATING DEALS

Second Listening: Write the number of the conversation beside each of the following expressions.

STATING THE PRICE

☐ Well, that'd be (I'd say) around fifty-five, sixty dollars.

☐ You're looking at about a hundred bucks, around there.

☐ It's $500 for a small one . . .

☐ That'll run you about $875

☐ I could do that for let's say seven hundred and fifty.

☐ I charge around $100 a room.

OFFERING DEALS

☐ I have special rates for seniors.

☐ It's regularly $10.00 but with this discount 25% (25% discount) that's only seven-fifty.

☐ Now, that's a good price!

☐ Let's say I do the whole shot for fifty.

☐ That's the best I can do for you, believe me.

☐ Actually, that's my specialty and I've got the best prices in the city.

☐ I could do that for the bargain price of let's say a hundred and twenty five bucks.

☐ You aren't going to find a better deal.

☐ I've got a special deal on houses right now.

☐ No GST.

HEDGING

☐ I don't know if I can afford that.

☐ Sounds good but I'm going to call around and see what other people are charging first.

☐ Let me talk to my wife and I'll call you back.

CLOSING THE DEAL

☐ I (I'd) say you've got a deal.

☐ OK, could you give me your name and address please?

☐ Is there any way you could do the job this afternoon?

☐ I'll be right there.

☐ That sounds reasonable.

SPEAKING WITH A PARTNER Here's your chance to negotiate deals. One person is Noel and the other is a customer. Use the price list and the expressions above to make up conversations.

CHAPTER 6: SPORTS

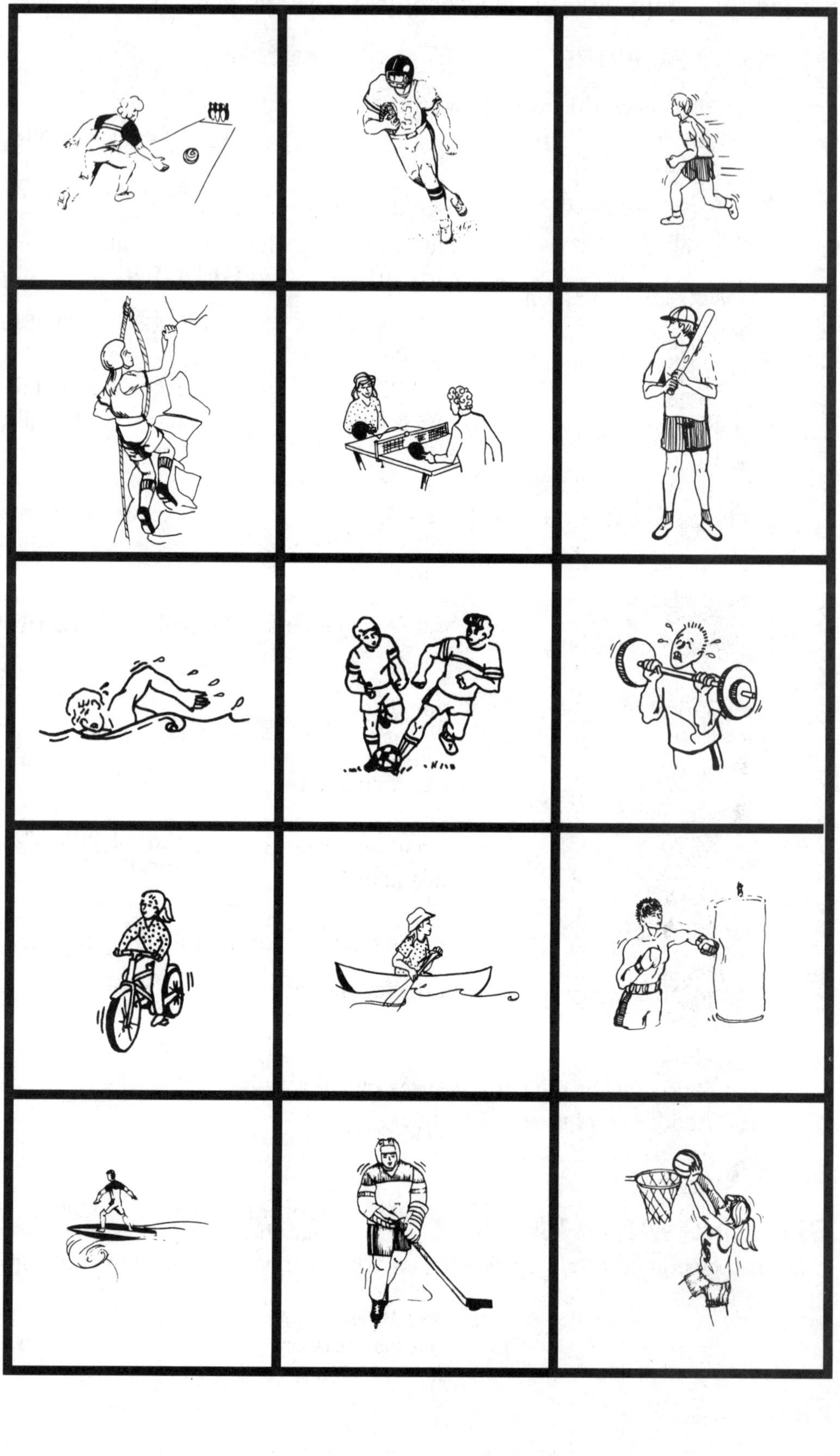

SPORTS

FACTS:

1. Seventy-five percent of Canadians are active in sports three times a week.

2. Men and women are equally active.

3. Walking is the favourite activity, followed by gardening, bicycling and swimming. Here are percentages showing Canadians' participation in sports:

walking	63%	golf	15%
gardening	52%	popular dance	13%
cycling	38%	baseball	11%
swimming	36%	downhill skiing	11%
home exercises	28%	ice hockey	11%
skating	21%	bowling	9%
jogging	18%	exercise classes (aerobics)	6%
cross country skiing	18%	racquetball	6%
tennis	15%	curling	5%

4. Active Canadians are usually
   -young
   -westerners
   -managers or professionals
   -single
   -well educated.

5. Canadians from B.C. are most active in sports. Quebeckers are the least active.

6. People exercise for the following reasons:

   (1) to feel better

   (2) for fun or excitement

   (3) to control weight

   (4) to relax.

7. The sale of sporting goods in Canada is over $2 billion a year.

**Instructor's Manual*
Sports quiz and discussion

LISTENING TO CANADIANS — PART 1

Before You Listen: Discuss the meaning of these words:

gym
professional
volleyball

team
coach
sailing

brought up
athlete
competition

Listen and fill in the missing information.

Jennifer Robinson, 17 Collingwood, Ont.

1. Favourite sport: ____________________
2. How often: ____________________

____

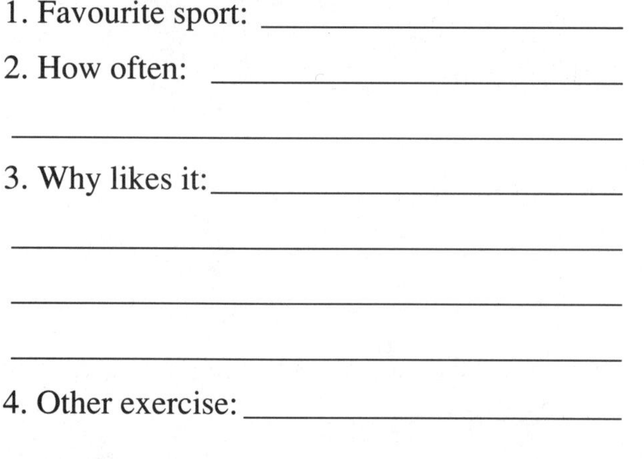

3. Why likes it: ____________________

____

____

____

4. Other exercise: ____________________

Stuart Cork, 29, Scarborough, Ont.

1. Favourite sport: ____________________
2. How often: ____________________

____

3. Why likes it: ____________________

____

____

____

4. Other exercise: ____________________

**Instructor's Manual*
Tapescript and discussion

LISTENING TO CANADIANS — PART 2

Before You Listen: Discuss the meaning of these words:

warm up	stretching	clears your mind
Toronto Maple Leafs	good shape	delivering mail

Listen and fill in the missing information.

Neeraja Vaid, 20, Vancouver, B.C

1. Favourite sport: ____________________
2. How often: ____________________

____

3. Why likes it: ____________________

____

____

____

4. Other exercise: ____________________

Gordon Lyons, 35, Toronto, Ont.

1. Favourite sport: ____________________
2. How often: ____________________

____

3. Why likes it: ____________________

____

____

____

4. Other exercise: ____________________

**Instructor's Manual*
Tapescript and discussion

Listening to the Story

LIFE OF A MOUNTAIN CLIMBER

First Listening: A magazine writer interviews Sharon Wood, the first Canadian woman to climb Mount Everest. Listen to their conversation and put the pictures in order.

Tell the story.

*Read it in *Amazing! Canadian Newspaper Stories.* Tapescript in *Instructor's Manual*

CORRECT THE REPORTER'S NOTES

Second Listening: Listen and correct the reporter's notes.
Mark an "x" beside anything that is wrong. Then listen again to correct the mistakes.

1. ☐ *born on Mount Everest*
2. ☐ *grew up in B.C.*
3. ☐ *five kids in family*
4. ☐ *she was oldest*
5. ☐ *liked staying indoors*
6. ☐ *loved animals*
7. ☐ *father liked climbing mountains*
8. ☐ *Sharon climbed rocks and hills as a child*
9. ☐ *quit school at seventeen*
10. ☐ *parents upset*
11. ☐ *started climbing at seventeen*
12. ☐ *Laurie Skreslet, the first Canadian to climb Everest, was her first climbing instructor*
13. ☐ *Laurie told her she needed to try harder if she wanted to be a good climber*
14. ☐ *started climbing in 1956 from the Tibet side*
15. ☐ *ten people all together*
16. ☐ *four people made it to the top*
17. ☐ *they didn't have enough oxygen for everyone to go to the top*
18. ☐ *in one way she felt good to be on top of the world*
19. ☐ *she was glad to get back home safely*

ASKING POLITELY

First Listening: A woman calls Golden Community Centre to find out about three courses. Listen and fill in the missing information on her "Things-To-Do" notepad.

THINGS TO DO	
Tennis classes	**Cooking classes**
levels: ____________	types: ____________
____________	____________
starts: ____________	instructor: ____________
day: ____________	when: ____________
# of weeks: ____________	starts: ____________
# of hrs. per lesson: ____________	# of weeks: ____________
how much: ____________	how much: ____________
Computer classes	**How to register**
____________	____________
____________	____________
____________	____________
____________	____________

Second Listening: Listen again and tick off [✔] the polite phrases you hear the woman use as she asks the receptionist for information.

1. ☐ I wonder
2. ☐ I am wondering
3. ☐ I was wondering
4. ☐ Can you tell me
5. ☐ Can you please tell me
6. ☐ Can you possibly tell me
7. ☐ Could you tell me
8. ☐ Could you please tell me
9. ☐ Could you possibly tell me
10 ☐ Would you mind telling me
11. ☐ I'd like to know
12. ☐ I want to know
13. ☐ I wanted to know
14. ☐ Do you know
15. ☐ Do you happen to know
16. ☐ Do you by any chance know
17. ☐ Do you have any idea
18. ☐ I am interested in knowing
19. ☐ I am interested in finding out
20. ☐ I was also interested in knowing
21. ☐ I was also interested in finding out

SPEAKING — CALLING FOR INFORMATION

PARTNER 1: Find out information about these courses by calling your partner who is the receptionist at Mountain College. Use the polite phrases from the last exercise to make questions.

> GRAMMAR RULE: Polite Questions
>
> Polite phrase + if/question word + subject + verb +...
> I want to know if you offer any computer courses.

ENGLISH CONVERSATION

levels: ______________________

when: ______________________

starts: ______________________

# of weeks: ______________________

# of hrs./lesson: ______________________

how much: ______________________

COMPUTER BASICS

types: ______________________

when: ______________________

starts: ______________________

# of weeks: ______________________

# of hrs./lesson: ______________________

how much: ______________________

WINE TASTING

levels: ______________________

when: ______________________

starts: ______________________

# of weeks: ______________________

hrs./lesson: ______________________

how much: ______________________

GRAMMAR REVIEW

levels: ______________________

when: ______________________

starts: ______________________

# of weeks: ______________________

hrs./lesson: ______________________

how much: ______________________

PARTNER 2: Turn to the next page.

SPEAKING — CALLING FOR INFORMATION

PARTNER 2: You are a receptionist at Mountain College. Use the list of courses below to help you answer your partner's questions.

GRAMMAR REVIEW
For ESL students or native speakers, these courses help you understand English grammar. ESL: Mon. 6:30-9:30 p.m. Jan. 26-Apr. 4. 8 wks. $150. Native Speakers, Tues.

ENGLISH CONVERSATION
Beginners, Intermediate and Advanced levels offered on Tues., Wed., and Fri. from 7:00-10:00 p.m. Jan. 28-May 15. 12 wks. $200.

WINE TASTING
Learn about the wines of the world. Beginners and Advanced courses. Beginners on Sat. Advanced on Sun. Jan. 31/Feb.1 - May 2/3. 6:30-9:30 p.m. 10 wks. $250. Wine provided.

COMPUTER BASICS
IBM and Apple courses for the beginner. Wed., Jan 27-Apr. 22. 7:00-10:00 p.m. 9 wks. $175.

EXTRA: Make a list of all the places in your area that offer ESL courses. Look up their phone numbers and call to find out when courses begin, how long they last, and how much they cost.

	Name of School	Phone	Starting date	How long	How much
1.					
2.					
3.					
4.					
5.					
6.					
7.					
8.					
9.					
10.					

CHAPTER 7: ADULT EDUCATION

Qin Mei Zhu, China

ADULT EDUCATION

FACTS: Part-time Courses

1. Twenty-one percent of women and 17% of men take part-time adult education courses every year.

2. Job-related courses are the most popular.

3. Young, single, university graduates are most likely to take a course.

4. Courses are usually about 61 hours and most are offered at night or on the weekends.

ESL Courses

5. The government is spending over $1 billion a year on English language training and immigrant services.

Literacy Courses

6. The government also puts aside money for the 5 000 000 Canadians who cannot read or write well enough to live a normal life in Canada.

7. Ten percent of Canadians cannot read directions on a medicine bottle.

8. Twenty percent can't find information in a newspaper article.

9. Thirty percent can't circle the long-distance charges on a telephone bill.

10. Forty percent can't figure out how much to tip for lunch in a restaurant.

11. Fifty percent have difficulty using a bus schedule.

12. The results of illiteracy are high unemployment, poor health, substance abuse, and problems with the law.

**Instructor's Manual*
Pre-reading activity and discussion

LISTENING TO CANADIANS — Interview 1

Before You Listen: 1. Discuss the meaning of these words:

accounting clerk kindergarten joking

2. Read the statements below. Ask about any words you don't know.

Listen and tick off [✓]all correct statements. Mark an "x" beside those that are wrong. Correct the mistakes.

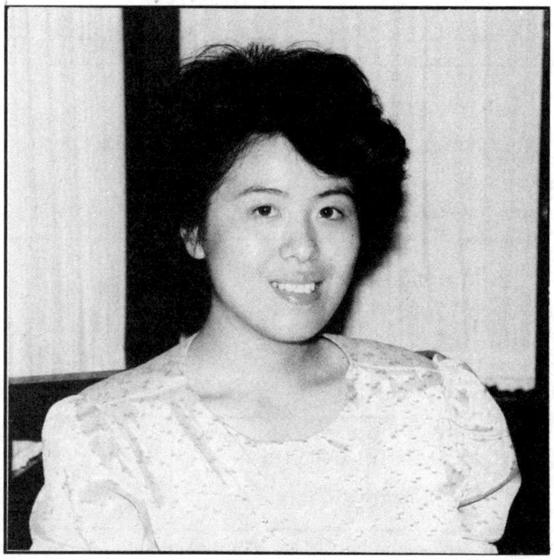

1. ☐ Mei completed high school.
2. ☐ Before in China, they could not study English.
3. ☐ She tried to learn English from TV, but finally returned to school.
4. ☐ Mei is taking part time English and full time computer courses.
5. ☐ She is taking Wordperfect 5.1, Lotus 1-2-3, and AccPac because she wants to go back to China.
6. ☐ Ms. Zhu plans to study English full-time for four years.

Qin Mei Zhu, 28, China

7. ☐ She was a factory worker in China.
8. ☐ She thinks learning a language is more difficult as an adult.
9. ☐ In China, students learn in a different way.
10. ☐ Here, everything is very serious and you cannot talk in English class.
11. ☐ She didn't like studying here at first, but now she likes it.
12. ☐ In China, studying is like playing games. Students have lots of fun in English class.
13. ☐ Mei thinks most students are lazy.
14. ☐ She likes school because it makes you study. It pushes you so you have to study.

LISTENING TO CANADIANS—Interview 2

Before You Listen: Discuss the meaning of these words:

welfare	upgrading	maintenance
foster home	sexual abuse	beating

Listen and write short answers.

Name: Place of Birth: Age: Education:	Inukassuk (Inuk) Frobisher Bay, Northwest Territories 43 years old completed Grade 3
1. Why did you return to school?	
2. What courses are you taking? (full or part time?)	
3. How long do you plan to study?	
4. What kind of work do you intend to get afterwards?	
5. Do you find it easier or more difficult to study as an adult?	
6. What do you like best about being back in school?	

**Instructor's Manual*
Tapescript and discussion

SPEAKING—ADULT EDUCATION AND YOU

Interview two of your classmates.

Name: Country of birth:		
1. How is studying in Canada different from studying in your country?		
2. What kind of adult education courses are there in your country?		
3. How long are you planning to study English? Why?		
4. Are you going to study full or part time?		
5. What kind of work would you like to do afterwards?		
6. Do you think it's easier or more difficult to study as an adult? Why?		
7. What do you like best about being in school? Why?		
8. What job-related courses would you like to take in the future? Why?		
9. What interest courses do you want to take? Why?		

ATIMA GETS AN EDUCATION

First Listening: A radio talk-show host is interviewing Atima, an Inuit man from the Northwest Territories. Listen to the interview and put the pictures in order.

Tell the story.

*Read it in *Amazing! Canadian Newspaper Stories.* Tapescript in *Instructor's Manual*

Listening to the Story—Atima Gets An Education

FILLING IN AN APPLICATION FORM

Second Listening: Fill in this application form for Atima.

JOB APPLICATION				
Family Name		Given Name(s)		
Address * * * * * * * * * * * * *				
City		Province/Territory		
Country		Postal Code * * * *		
Single ☐	Married ☐	Divorced ☐	Separated ☐	Other ☐
Last Grade Completed 1 2 3 4 5 6 7 8 9 10 11 12 13 14				
Type of Job Preferred				
Reason for Leaving Last Job				
Languages Spoken		Languages Written		
References—Name	Position		Years Known	
Address * * * *		Phone * * * *		

Reacting to the Story—Atima Gets An Education

APPLICATION FORMS AND ADULT-EDUCATION FLYERS

Contact Assignment 1: Go to places you might like to work and ask for application forms. Bring back as many forms as possible to share with your classmates.

Contact Assignment 2: Go to colleges, high schools and community centres to find out what adult-education courses they offer. Ask for their flyers. Share the information with your classmates.

SETTING UP A JOB INTERVIEW

First Listening: You will hear three people call to set up job interviews. Circle the newspaper ads they are calling about and write the number of the conversation inside each circle.

HELP WANTED	HELP WANTED
TV movie needs extras m/f. Male orientals 18-25 also req'd. Action Studios, 875-8775	Busy school photography company req's a f/t photographer. Must be good with children. 992-8383
F/T STORE DETECTIVE experience preferred, good salary and benefits. 326-4662	F/t & p/t cashiers needed for self-serve gas station. Students welcome. 999-9292
WAITER/WAITRESS for busy restaurant. Eve. shifts. F/t & p/t. 737-7337	COURIER DRIVERS m/f full-time, must have good knowledge of city. $2000./mo. 873-6336

Second Listening: Write the number of the conversation beside each question or answer.

SAYING YOU DON'T UNDERSTAND

☐ I'm sorry, I didn't understand that.

☐ I'm afraid I missed that.

☐ Hey, sorry, I didn't follow that exactly.

☐ I'm sorry, I didn't get that.

ASKING FOR REPETITION

☐ Would you mind repeating that?

☐ Uh, what was your question?

☐ Excuse me, could you repeat that last part?

☐ You're having what?

ASKING FOR SPELLING

☐ Would you mind spelling that for me?

SPEAKING WITH A PARTNER

Practice calling to set up a job interview. Be sure to get the correct date, time, and address. Use the newspaper ads on this page or bring in your own from a local newspaper. If you don't understand something the boss or receptionist says, use the expressions above.

EMPLOYMENT

FACTS:

1. Sixty-five percent of those aged 15 and older are in the labour force—12,176,000 are employed, and 1,511,000 are unemployed. Seven million, four hundred, and ninety-seven thousand are not in the labour force: they are neither working nor collecting unemployment insurance.
2. Last year the government paid out $17.7 billion in UIC benefits.
3. The number of people in the labour force is increasing every year. There was a large increase in the '70s because baby boomers started working. A continuous increase in the number of women working is another reason that there are more people in the labour force every year.
4. Women's participation in the labour force has increased from 38% to 58% in the last twenty years. Over the same 20 years, men's participation has declined from 78% to 77%.
5. Sixty-nine percent of mothers with children under 16 years old work. This is up from 49% ten years ago.
6. Sixty-two percent of families have two incomes. Their combined average income is $50,000, with women making $14,000 or 29% of the total income.
7. In the last ten years women's full-time earnings have increased 8% whereas men's earnings over the same period have declined 1%.
8. Women earn 70% of what men earn at all educational levels. There is evidence that this is changing because women aged 25-34 with a university degree now make 80% of males with the same qualifications.
9. The labour force is aging. The average age of (participants) workers is 36.3 today and was 35.5 ten years ago.
10. Workers are better educated than they were ten years ago. Today 15% have a university degree and 42% have some post-secondary education. A decade ago only 10% of workers had a university degree and just 29% had post-secondary education.
11. Part-time work has increased. Today 15% of employed people (22% of women, 9% of men) work part time; fifteen years ago only 11% had part-time jobs.
12. The service industries (including hotel and food services, wholesale and retail sales, insurance, real estate, finance, education, health and welfare, recreation, transportation, communication, and utilities) have expanded. More than 2/3 of all workers are employed in a service position.

13. The economy is divided into two sectors: the service sector and the goods producing sector (including agriculture, manufacturing, construction, mining, forestry, and fishing). During the last ten years the service sector has grown 29%; the goods-producing sector has grown only 4%.
14. Almost 3/4 of women employed outside the home worked in traditional female positions: clerical jobs, service, sales, nursing and other health occupations, or teaching.
15. In the last ten years there has been a small decrease in the number of women choosing these traditional occupations: 77% vs 72%.
16. The following information shows the percentage of women employed in a variety of occupations:

nursing	85%	sales	46%
clerical	80%	managerial/administrative	38%
teaching	66%	manufacturing	20%
social sciences	57%	transportation	9%
service	57%	construction	2%

17. The following table shows the percent of men and women employed in various types of occupations:

	men	women
managerial/professional/technical	24%	29%
clerical	7%	31%
sales	8%	10%
service	13%	18%
primary (farming, mining, etc.)	5%	1%
processing	20%	6%
construction	11%	1%
transportation	6%	1%
material handling	6%	2%
	100%	100%

18. The following chart shows the average weekly earnings and hours of work for a number of employment categories:

	weekly earnings	weekly hours
mines	$940	40.6
construction	$651	35.6
goods producing	$677	37.9
finance	$575	24.2
manufacturing	$658	38.2
trade/sales	$395	—
transportation	$689	36.5
community/business services	$480	26.3

19. Thirty-four percent of all workers are unionized. Average weekly earnings for unionized workers is $611 for males and $429 for females. Non-unionized men make $410; women earn $283.

**Instructor's Manual:* Pre-reading activity and discussion
Alternate Activity: Have students compare these facts with information about employment in their countries.

CHAPTER 8: SENIOR CITIZENS

Gerald Deines, Toronto, Ont.

Marion Cameron, Niagara Falls, Ont.

Canadian Culture—Senior Citizens

FACTS:

1. Twelve percent of Canadians are over 65 years old.
2. By 2031, one in four or 25% of Canadians will be senior citizens.
3. Most seniors live in single detached homes.
4. Two-thirds have automobiles and cable television.
5. Seniors get most of their money from government pensions — Old Age Security and Guaranteed Income Supplement.
6. To get OAS, you must live in Canada for at least ten years and sometimes longer. To get GIS, you need to have a low income.
7. Most seniors live alone.
8. Eleven percent don't speak English or French.
9. Seniors smoke less than younger people:
   19% over 65 smoke,
   37% under 55 smoke.
10. Older men drink more than younger men, but women of all ages drink the same amount.

	Men	Women
25-44	15% drink daily	5% drink daily
65-80	20% drink daily	5% drink daily

11. More seniors exercise regularly now than they did six years ago.
12. Fifty-eight percent of seniors travel for enjoyment.
13. Sixty-one percent go out to public places like movie theatres and restaurants.
14. About one quarter take part in activities like bingo, card games or courses.
15. Seventy-nine percent read one or more newspapers a week.
16. Seniors watch more TV and spend a longer time reading than most adults. This is because they have 7.7 hours of free time every day while other adults only have 5.5.
17. Forty-four percent of seniors participate in sports or have a hobby.
18. Seniors sleep longer than young people (8.7 vs. 8.1 hours).

**Instructor's Manual*
Pre-reading activity and discussion
Alternate Activity: Have students compare these facts with information about seniors in their countries.

LISTENING TO CANADIANS — Interview 1

Before You Listen: 1. Discuss the meaning of these words:

Easterner	Liquor Control Board (LCBO)	pension
smuggling	Dominican Republic	roll over
cost of living	touch wood	it depends

2. What questions will the interviewer ask?

Listen and fill in the missing information.

1. What's it like: ______________________

____

____

____

____

2. Keep busy: ______________________

____

____

____

Gerald Deines, 66, Toronto, Ont.

3. Now versus ten or twenty years ago: ______________________

____

4. Secret to long life: ______________________

____

____

5. Happiest time: ______________________

____

6. Secret to happiness: ______________________

____

____

7. Plans for future: ______________________

____

LISTENING TO CANADIANS—Interview 2

Before You Listen: 1. Discuss the meaning of these words:

B.C. coast	live moderately	stand out in your mind
graduating	Pakistan	carry on

2. What questions will the interviewer ask?

Listen and fill in the missing information.

1. What's it like: ______

2. Keep busy: ______

Marion Cameron, 68, Niagara Falls, Ont.

3. Now versus ten or twenty years ago: ______

4. Secret to living a long life: ______

5. Happiest time: ______

6. Secret to happiness: ______

7. Plans for the future: ______

**Instructor's Manual*
Tapescript and discussion

SPEAKING — INTERVIEW A SENIOR

Talk to a "golden ager" and use the information to write a story.

1. What's your name? ______________________________
____
2. Where are you from? ______________________________
____
3. What's it like being a senior citizen in Canada? ______________________________
____
4. What do you do to keep busy? ______________________________
____
____
5. What is the secret to living a long life?
____
____
____
6. How is your life different now than it was ten or twenty years ago? ______________________________
____
____
7. What was the happiest time in your life? ______________________________
____
____
8. What is the secret to happiness? ______________________________
____
____
____

CLASS DISCUSSION

1. How old is the oldest person in your family?
2. What do you remember about your grandparents?
3. What is the secret to living a long life?
4. How long do you want to live?
5. What would you like to do before you die?

Listening to the Story

100-YEAR-OLD COMES TO CANADA

First Listening: A newspaper reporter is interviewing Maria in her home. Listen to their conversation and put the pictures in order.

Tell the story.

* Read it in *Amazing! Canadian Newspaper Stories.*
Tapescript in *Instructor's Manual*

CORRECT THE REPORTER'S NOTES

Second Listening: Read over the reporter's notes and listen again to correct any errors. Mark an "x" beside anything that is wrong, and correct the mistakes.

1. ☐ *Mrs. Rozario is the oldest person to immigrate to Canada.*
2. ☐ *She was born in 1990.*
3. ☐ *She came to Vancouver to be with her husband.*
4. ☐ *He was a Portuguese businessman.*
5. ☐ *Maria met him in Portugal.*
6. ☐ *She is from Kowloon, Hong Kong.*
7. ☐ *She lives in the Happy Tattoo House.*
8. ☐ *There are lots of people in Hong Kong.*
9. ☐ *Maria immigrated to Canada because she wanted a vegetable garden.*
10. ☐ *She also wanted to be with her thirty children.*
11. ☐ *She started working at forty.*
12. ☐ *She was the secretary for seven bosses at the same time.*
13. ☐ *She is happy to be back together with her children and great grandchildren.*
14. ☐ *She fought in the First and Second World Wars.*
15. ☐ *She likes communism.*
16. ☐ *She is over one hundred years old.*
17. ☐ *She drinks a bottle of brandy every day.*
18. ☐ *She says the secret to living a long life is to drink brandy every day and to eat everything, especially vegetables.*

REMEMBER WHEN...

First Listening: Write the number of the monologue beside the correct picture.

I REMEMBER

Second Listening: Listen again and write the number of the monologue beside an expression for talking about the past. Only nine of the following expressions are in the monologues.

☐ If I remember correctly...

☐ When I was younger...

☐ If I think back...

☐ I can remember...

☐ A long time ago...

☐ ...was something I used to think about a lot.

☐ Ages ago...

☐ I remember...

☐ Way back...

☐ I often think about that time.

☐ I'll always remember...

☐ When I think of it now...

☐ It happened a number of years back.

☐ That's something I'll never forget.

☐ It really stands out in my mind.

☐ I remember it as clearly as if it were yesterday.

☐ Back then...

☐ That really brings back memories.

SPEAKING

1. Tell your partner about your most memorable experience.
2. Tell your partner what you remember about your grandparents.
3. Tell your partner what you remember about your childhood.
4. Tell your partner what you remember about life in your country.

CHAPTER 9: FREE-TIME ACTIVITIES

Canadian Culture

FREE-TIME ACTIVITIES

FACTS:

1. Canadians spend an average of five and a half hours a day on free-time activities.

2. People watch TV or rent movies for about two hours and fifteen minutes a day. (They also watch for another hour but are busy doing something else at the same time.)

3. Socializing with others–visiting friends and relatives or talking on the phone–takes up about an hour a day.

4. Adults spend around 45 minutes a day on sports and hobbies. The five most popular sports are cycling, swimming, skating, jogging, and cross country skiing. (See Chapter 6 for the complete list.)

5. Other entertainment activities like going to movies take up about half an hour.

6. Canadians spend about 30 minutes a day reading.

7. When Canadians were asked what they would like to do if they were left alone on a desert island:
   - 70% said they would like to spend the time with their spouse (husband or wife) or an attractive member of the opposite sex;
   - 14% said they would want a library of all the books they ever wanted to read;
   - 6% said they would like a TV set with all the channels and extra videos; and
   - 3% said they would like all the music they could ever want to listen to.

**Instructor's Manual*
Pre-reading activity and discussion

LISTENING TO CANADIANS — Part 1

First Listening: Listen to three people—Kim, Joseph, and Susan—talk about their free-time activities. Write their first initial, K, J, or S, beside the activities each person talks about. If two people do the same activity, write two initials.

1. ________ go to movies
2. ________ cleaning the house
3. ________ cross-country skiing
4. ________ curling
5. ________ go to a summer cottage
6. ________ baseball
7. ________ look after the house (cleaning, fixing, repairing)
8. ________ look at garage sales and antique stores
9. ________ play tennis
10. ________ read
11. ________ do aerobics, exercise, keep in shape
12. ________ relax
13. ________ have friends over
14. ________ spend time with the family
15. ________ swimming
16. ________ biking (cycling)
17. ________ walking
18. ________ snowmobiling

Susan Cork, 28, Scarborough, Ont.

Speaking—Interviewing

What questions did the interviewer ask? Ask your partner the same questions and share the answers with the class.

**Instructor's Manual*
Tapescript and discussion

LISTENING TO CANADIANS — Part 2

Second Listening: Listen again and write short answers.

Name: From: Age:	Kim Vaillant Sudbury, Ont. 19 years old	Joseph Tomlin St. Catharines, Ont. 72 years old	Susan Cork Scarborough, Ont. 28 years old
1. How many hours a week do you work/ go to school?			
2. What do you like doing in your free time?			
3. What do you usually do in the evenings?			
4. What do you do on the weekends?			
5. Do you do different things at different times of the year? Explain.			
6. Would you like to have more free time? Why or why not?			

Which person walks alone at night? Why?
Are you afraid to walk alone at night in your neighbourhood? Why or why not?

Listening to the Story

CANADIAN LEARNS CHINESE

First Listening: Two parents are talking about Michael, who lives down the street. Listen and put the pictures in order.

Tell the story.

*Read it in *Amazing! Canadian Newspaper Stories.*

NEIGHBOURS

Second Listening: Listen again and fill in the missing words.

(M = man; W = woman)

M: You know Michael, that kid down the ____________.[1]

W: Oh yeah. Sure, uh I know him. He ____________ [2] to Ottawa High with my son.

M: Well he had his picture in the ____________ [3] yesterday.

W: Really! And uh why was that?

M: It said that he ____________[4] to speak Chinese!

W: Chinese! You're kidding!

M: No. Apparently he started studying ____________[5] years ago...

W: Really!

M: ...on the weekends.

W: Hmmmm. I guess he ____________[6] a challenge, eh?

M: Well, I guess so. Uh, it said he went to language classes in the ____________[7]...

W: Uh-huh.

M: ...and in the afternoon he learned about culture...

W: Uh?

M: ...the Chinese culture.

W: What do you ____________?[8]

M: Culture, you know, like uh, he learned about the people, their crafts, uh their,[9] uh you know...

W: Mmm, what kind of sports?

M: Ping-pong.

W: Ah, like table ____________[10] you mean?

M: Yeah, and kung-fu.

W: So Michael can do kung-fu, eh?

M: That's ____________[11] it said.

W: Yeah, uh-huh. But did he really learn Chinese or...

M: Apparently! It said that he knows 2000 different symbols and can ____________[12] 1000.

W: Amazing! But can he speak it?

M: Oh yeah. He learned new words with his Chinese-English ____________.[13] His teachers made him tapes. Uh, I think he graduated with a seventy-five.

W: Hey, that's not too bad.

M: I'd say it's pretty good. You know, he was the first one, the first non-Chinese student to ____________[14] from the school.

W: Hmmm!

M: And that's not all.

W: There's more?

M: Yeah, they told about Michael's other ____________[15] too!

W: You mean he has time for other things!

M: Sure. He studies French, uh he ____________,[16] a little German, plays the recorder, collects stamps and coins, and he's interested in science.

W: ____________[17] amazing!

MAKING SUGGESTIONS/GIVING ADVICE

First Listening: You will hear Michael give advice to four people who have problems. Write the number of the conversation beside the correct problem.

☐ A student just moved into the neighbourhood and doesn't know anyone.

☐ A female ESL student is having trouble learning English.

☐ A friend is bored and doesn't know what to do in his free time.

☐ His best friend can't get a date with a girl.

CAN I MAKE A SUGGESTION?

Second Listening: Listen again and write the number of the conversation beside expressions for giving advice.

- [ ] You've really got to...
- [ ] Can I make a suggestion?
- [ ] Why don't you...
- [ ] I think you should...
- [ ] You could always...
- [ ] Why don't we...
- [ ] How about...
- [ ] I (really) think you ought to...
- [ ] If I were you, I'd...
- [ ] Can I give you a piece of advice?
- [ ] You might try...

Can you think of any other ways to give advice? Write them here:

______________________ ______________________

______________________ ______________________

______________________ ______________________

SPEAKING — "DEAR MICHAEL,..."

Michael works for the school newspaper. He writes an advice column. Here is one of the letters he received.

> Dear Michael,
>
> I have a big problem. I'm pregnant and no one knows but me. I'm sixteen and my boyfriend is eighteen. What should I do?
>
> Signed: Upset

WORK IN SMALL GROUPS

1. Discuss this problem and try to use some of the expressions for giving advice.
2. Write your group's answer on the blackboard. (Dear Upset,...) Discuss the problem with the class.
3. Change groups and work together to make up a problem. Write it on the board. Discuss the problems with the class. Offer your advice.

CHAPTER 10: THE ENVIRONMENT

Sean Delaney, Yellowknife, NWT

Jack Gray, Toronto, Ont.

Canadian Culture

FACTS:

1. Ninety-five percent of Canadians are worried about the environment.

2. Canadians are worried about:
   a) unclean drinking water
   b) pollution of lakes and rivers
   c) acid rain (chemical waste returning to earth as rain)
   d) spills of dangerous materials
   e) industrial and chemical waste
   f) air pollution.

3. Seventy-one percent of people buy "environmentally friendly" products.

4. Many Canadians are becoming green activists—they are doing something about the problems of the environment by:
   a) using recycled goods
   b) not buying aerosol cans or foods packaged in plastic or styrofoam
   c) recycling cans, bottles, and paper

d) boycotting (not buying) products of polluting companies
e) using unleaded gas.

5. Green activists are more likely to live in Alberta, B.C., or Ontario, have university educations, be middle-aged, and earn high salaries.

6. One in six Canadian households drinks bottled or purified water. One in three Montreal households drinks it. Why? Because half the sewage in Montreal—a city of over 2 000 000—is dumped directly into the St. Lawrence River.

7. The drinking water in Toronto contains 50 different things that are bad for your health—16 of them cause cancer.

8. Eighty-four percent of Canadians want mandatory (you have to do it) recycling.

9. Sixty-seven percent would like to see fewer cars on the road.

10. Three quarters of all Canadians want all sales of plastic and foam to stop.

11. Fifty-four percent would like a $100 extra charge on income tax to help protect the environment.

12. Eighty-five percent think the government is not doing enough to protect the environment.

13. Canadians produce more waste per person than any other country in the world. We produce 1.8 kg of waste per person per day, while Americans produce 1.6 kg.

14. Around 1.5 million animals are trapped every year for the fur trade.

15. One in 40 of the animals in Canada is on the endangered species list.

16. Through working to protect the environment, Canada has become one of the first countries to take animals off their endangered species list.

**Instructor's Manual*
Pre-reading activity, true/false quiz and discusssion

LISTENING TO CANADIANS — Getting Ready

Before You Listen: You will hear three Canadians talk about environmental problems and what individuals can do. They will also talk about hunting and endangered species. Discuss these questions with the class and write out the answers.

1. What environmental problems do you think they will talk about?

a) ______________________________

b) ______________________________

c) ______________________________

d) ______________________________

e) ______________________________

f) ______________________________

g) ______________________________

2. What will they say we can do to help?

a) ______________________________

b) ______________________________

c) ______________________________

d) ______________________________

e) ______________________________

f) ______________________________

g) ______________________________

3. What will they say about hunting and trapping?

a) ______________________________

b) ______________________________

First Listening: Circle the letter if they talk about what the class thought they would discuss.

LISTENING TO CANADIANS — Interview 1

Before You Listen: Discuss the meaning of these words:

industrial and chemical waste	corporations	products
holes in the ozone layer	survival	endangered species
way of life	trapping	native population

Listen and fill in the missing information.

1. Environmental problems: ______________________

____

____

____

____

Sean Delaney, 26, Yellowknife, NWT

2. What can individuals do? ______________________

____

____

____

____

____

3. Do we have the right to hunt and kill animals? ______________________

____

____

____

4. Should we protect certain animals? ______________________

____

DISCUSSION

1. Do you think people should stop driving automobiles?
2. Why are holes in the ozone layer a problem?
3. Do you think we have the right to hunt and kill animals for food and clothing?
4. Do you agree with Sean that it is all right for the native population to hunt and kill animals but that other Canadians should not do this?

LISTENING TO CANADIANS — Interview 2

Before You Listen: 1. Discuss the meaning of these words:

recycling | take seriously | waste

2. Read the statements below. Ask about any words you don't know.

Listen and tick off [✔] all correct statements. Mark an "x" beside those that are wrong. Correct the mistakes.

1. ☐ Jack thinks the biggest environmental problem we face today is our garbage.
2. ☐ He says our landfill sites are nearly all filled up and there is no place to put all the garbage.
3. ☐ The big thing Canadians can do to help is write letters to the government.
4. ☐ He thinks there is too much packaging in the products we use every day.
5. ☐ He says manufacturers can help out by using plastic, not paper.
6. ☐ Jack says we need to control hunting.
7. ☐ He says hunting is a sport for the rich.
8. ☐ He thinks hunting should be allowed for the rich and the poor.
9. ☐ He says that animals on the endangered species list have to be protected.

Jack Gray, 37, Toronto, Ont.

DISCUSSION

1. What does Jack mean when he says, "There is far too much packaging and waste."
2. Are manufacturers doing anything about this problem?
3. Jack says we should take recycling very seriously. Do you take it seriously? If yes, give examples.
4. What do you think of people who hunt and kill animals?

LISTENING TO CANADIANS — Interview 3

Before You Listen: Discuss the meaning of these words:

industrial/chemical waste	dumping	polluted	St. Lawrence
stored or destroyed	laws	tuna	dolphins
environmentally friendly	balance	phosphate free	depend on

Listen and write short answers.

Name: From: Age:	Marifrance Charette Montreal, Quebec 27 years old
1. What environmental problems do you know about?	
2. What can individuals do to help?	
3. Do we have the right to hunt and kill for food and clothing?	
4. Should we protect certain animals?	

**Instructor's Manual*
Tapescript and discussion

"SAVE OUR ENVIRONMENT" POSTER

IN SMALL GROUPS Design a poster showing environmental problems and things we can do to help. Use the spaces below to help you decide what information to include on your poster.

ENVIRONMENTAL PROBLEMS	WHAT YOU CAN DO

Practice here:

Now draw your poster on large paper or on the blackboard.

LORETTA LOBSTER FLIES HOME

First Listening: A TV talk-show host is interviewing Wylie about Loretta. Listen to their conversation and put the pictures in order.

Tell the story.

*Read it in *Amazing! Canadian Newspaper Stories.*
Tapescript in *Instructor's Manual*

PERSUADING

First Listening: You will hear three conversations. Write the number of the conversation beside what each conversation is about.

☐ Wylie tries to persuade a restaurant manager to buy lobsters.

☐ Wylie tries to persuade his wife to clean the house.

☐ Canadian Airlines persuades Wylie to fly to Nova Scotia with Loretta.

☐ Someone tries to persuade Wylie to sell Loretta.

Second Listening: Here are some phrases used to persuade. Listen to the conversations and complete the sentences.

CONVERSATION 1

Persuading

1. I really think you should ______________________________.
2. Besides, ______________________________.
3. And listen to this, ______________________________.
4. If you ______________________________,
   we ______________________________.
5. It's a bargain, ______________________________.
6. And another thing, ______________________________.

Giving In

1. All right. You twisted ______________________________.

Extra

How did Wylie use the example of Fred's restaurant to persuade the restaurant manager?

____

CONVERSATION 2

Persuading

1. It'd be great if ______________________________.
2. Oh come on now, ______________________________
   ______________________________.
3. This would really mean a lot ______________________________.
4. Let's say I give you ______________________________.
5. I'll give you ______________________________.

6. Now is that a generous offer ______________________________?

CONVERSATION 3

Persuading

1. ______________________________ good news for you.
2. We thought you might like ______________________________.
3. We think it's a good idea because ______________________________
______________________________.
4. And besides, ______________________________.
5. And as an added bonus ______________________________
______________________________.
6. And of course, you'll get ______________________________.
7. What else can we do ______________________________?

Giving In

1. You drive ______________________________.
2. You've got a ______________________________.
3. You scratch my back, ______________________________.

Extra

What does Wylie persuade Canadian Airlines to do?

____

SPEAKING IN PAIRS

1. Practice the conversations above. First read the tapescript, and then practice each conversation using the conversation topic and completed expressions as a guide.
2. Do you know other expressions for "persuading" and "giving in"? Use all of the expressions you know to practice the following conversations.

A woman is persuading her husband to cook dinner.	A salesclerk is persuading a woman to buy a dress and shoes.	A man is persuading his daughter to stop smoking.
A father is persuading his son to finish his homework.	A car salesperson is persuading a newlywed couple to buy a car.	A woman is persuading her neighbour to babysit her children.
A student is persuading the teacher to lend him/her money.	A woman is persuading her friend to help her move.	A son is persuading his mother to let him borrow the car.

CHAPTER 11: GIVING BIRTH

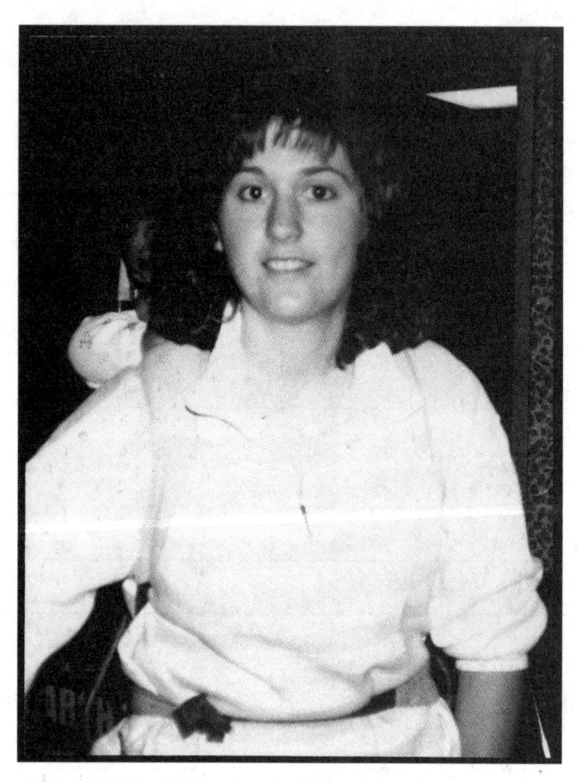

Amanda McCullough, Maple Ridge, B.C.

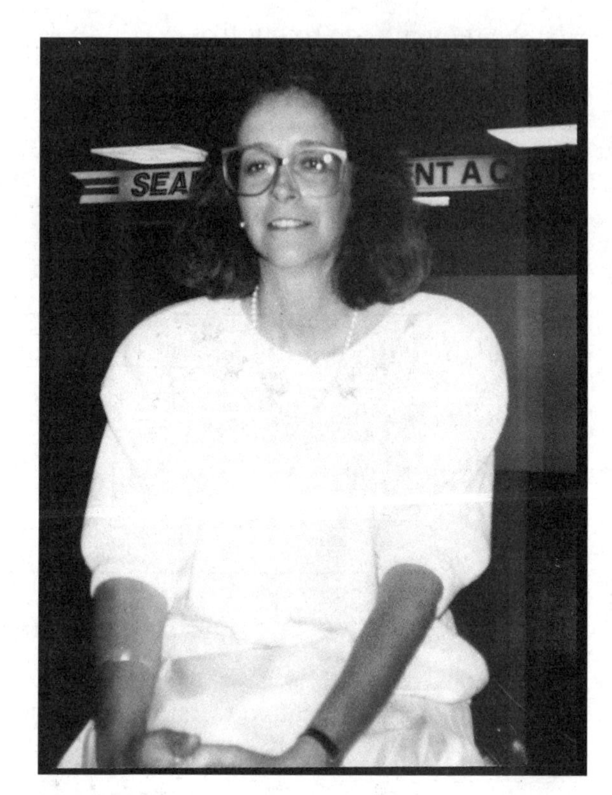

Danielle Poirier, Quebec City, Que.

Canadian Culture

GIVING BIRTH

FACTS:

1. Women around the world are having fewer and fewer children and the same is true in Canada.
2. Around 30 years ago, women were having around 4 children each. Today they are having 1.7. Women in Quebec are only having 1.4.
3. Women wait longer to have their first child and space their children further apart.
4. More parents are becoming first-time parents in their late 20s and early 30s.
5. One out of three children is born to a mother 30 years or older.
6. There are around 375 000 live births in Canada every year.
7. More than half of these babies are born in Ontario and Quebec.
8. Most women today give birth for the first time at 26 years of age.
9. The number of unmarried women having children is three times higher than it was 10 years ago.
10. Ninety-nine percent of babies are born in hospitals.
11. Fathers can go into the labour room 98% of the time. Children can go in during labour in only 27% of hospitals. Grandparents are allowed in 56% of the time.
12. People are allowed to room-in with mothers only during the day.
13. Eighty percent of mothers breast-feed their children.
14. A baby girl born today will usually live almost 80 years. A boy will live around 73 years.
15. Eleven percent of 18-34 year olds don't have or don't want to have children. Fifteen percent of college women feel this way.
16. The favourite birth control method is the pill (39%); next is sterilization (30%).
17. In Quebec, half of the women over 40 are sterilized.
18. Forty-four percent of Canadians think the pill is safe for women's health. Thirty-nine percent think it's not safe, and 17% are unsure.

**Instructor's Manual*
Pre-reading activity and discussion
Alternate Activity: Discuss how these facts compare with information about giving birth in your students' countries.

LISTENING TO CANADIANS — Interview 1

Before You Listen: 1. Discuss the meaning of these words:

anaesthetic breathing inhuman

2. Read the statements below. Ask about any words you don't know.

Listen and tick off [✔] all correct statements. Mark an "x" beside those that are wrong. Correct the mistakes.

1. ☐ Danielle has given birth four times.
2. ☐ The births were wonderful!
3. ☐ She gave birth to normal children.
4. ☐ Danielle had natural childbirth with no medication.
5. ☐ She was in labour twenty hours the first time and ten minutes the second.
6. ☐ The hospital staff were specially trained to help women who wanted to have natural childbirth.
7. ☐ Danielle had cravings for ice cream with pizza.
8. ☐ She ate more when she was with her husband.
9. ☐ Her husband didn't help.
10. ☐ She went to five pre-natal classes.
11. ☐ The classes were helpful for her husband.
12. ☐ She thinks mothers should have the choice of giving birth at home or in the hospital.
13. ☐ She thinks natural childbirth is wonderful.
14. ☐ She feels that she was lucky to be able to have natural childbirth because sometimes labour is too painful and too long.
15. ☐ She thinks women should have a caesarean after sixteen hours of pain.
16. ☐ She is sure that no man would suffer the pain of childbirth.

Amanda McCullough, 26, Maple Ridge, B.C.

LISTENING TO CANADIANS — Interview 2

Before You Listen: 1. Discuss the meaning of these words:

delivery　　That's average.　　nutrition　　equipment

2. What questions will the interviewer ask? **Listen** and fill in the missing information.

1. Number of births: ______________________
2. Giving birth was: ______________________

____

____

3. Labour: ______________________

____

4. Hospital staff: ______________________

____

____

5. Cravings: ______________________

____

Danielle Poirier, 36, Quebec City, Que.

6. Gain weight: ______________________

____

7. Husband help: ______________________

____

____

8. Pre-natal classes: ______________________

____

____

____

8. Home or hospital: ______________________

____

9. Natural childbirth: ______________________

____

____

**Instructor's Manual*: Tapescript and discussion

CHILDBIRTH AROUND THE WORLD

Ask questions to two students from different countries.

Name: Country:	
1. How many children do women usually have in your country?	
2. At what age do women usually first give birth?	
3. Do parents attend pre-natal classes? How many? What do they learn?	
4. Where do women usually give birth?	
5. Are others allowed in the delivery room? Who?	
6. How much do men help out during pregnancy and childbirth?	
7. Do people practice natural childbirth?	
8. Do mothers breast-feed their children?	
9. Do men and women get time off work after a child is born? How much? Paid?	
10. Can parents have as many children as they want?	
11. What do people think of an unmarried pregnant woman?	
12. What kinds of birth control are popular?	

Discuss your answers with the class.

911 FOR DELIVERY

First Listening: Sharon and Robert are having a dinner party and are telling their friends how Robert helped deliver their new baby. Listen to the conversation and put the pictures in order.

Tell the story.

*Instructor's Manual
Tapescript

CORRECT THE MISTAKES

Second Listening: Listen again and correct the errors in this newspaper article.

911 FOR DELIVERY

Last night, Sharon Reid went into labour at 12:30 p.m. Her husband, Robert, called 911 for BBQ chicken and the emergency operator told him to move Sharon into a chair and call back when he could see the baby's feet.

A few minutes later, the baby's toes showed and Sharon was screaming, "I'm not going to make it. I'm not going to make it." Robert was "freaking out" because the chicken wasn't there and he didn't know what to do.

He dialled 911 again and the same operator answered. The man told Robert to put his hands on the baby's head but not to pull it.

Robert's brother, Jim, was helping out now. He was on the phone and telling Robert what to do. She told him to grab the legs and keep the baby's head down. Then she told him to clean the baby's mouth out with a clean towel.

Robert started yelling, "It's a girl! It's a girl!" and everyone was congratulating everyone else.

A few minutes later the ambulance arrived and the attendants rushed in. They helped Sharon and cut the umbilical cord.

When they handed the baby back to Robert, he was a little surprised because it wasn't a girl, it was a boy!

Both Robert and Sharon are very happy with their new baby and named her Montana—an unusual name for an unusual birth.

GIVING INSTRUCTIONS

First Listening: Parents are telling a babysitter what she has to do. Listen and complete the list of instructions on this "Things To Do" notepad.

THINGS TO DO

Feed baby:

Bottle:

Diapers:

Burp:

Dinner for kids:

TV:

Bedtime: Jamie —

Claire —

Piano:

Colours:

Medicine:

Homework:

Extra

Why does the babysitter ask how much she is going to get paid?

____

____

WE WANT YOU TO...

Second Listening: Listen again and tick off [✔] the expressions you hear for giving instructions.

1. ☐ Don't let them...
2. ☐ Make sure...
3. ☐ You'd better...
4. ☐ We want you to...
5. ☐ We need you to...
6. ☐ You might want to...
7. ☐ She has to...
8. ☐ Don't forget to...
9. ☐ You need to...
10. ☐ You can let Jamie...
11. ☐ You should...
12. ☐ You'll have to...
13. ☐ You have to...
14. ☐ You've got to...
15. ☐ Tell them to...
16. ☐ Make them...

SPEAKING — GIVING INSTRUCTIONS

Use the expressions above to practice these conversations with different partners. One person is the parent and the other is the babysitter.

Feed five children at 6 o'clock Clean up the kitchen afterwards Tell kids to clean their rooms Turn off the TV after 8:00 p.m. Correct everyone's homework Give Steven his medicine Take out the garbage Put kids to bed at 9:00 p.m.	Give dog a bath Order out for pizza Tip the driver Read kids a story before bed Go to the park after dinner with children Buy them ice cream on the way home Put them to bed by ten
Feed twins every two hours Use cloth diapers in cupboard Do the laundry if you run out Sing to the babies if they cry Pay the newspaper delivery boy Don't play the stereo too loud Make yourself dinner Put them to bed at 6:30 p.m.	Make dinner with children Go swimming together in the outdoor pool Help them with their homework Take them for a drive Don't let them eat any candy Watch videos before bed Bed at 10:00 p.m.

CHAPTER 12: FRENCH AND ENGLISH CANADA

Jean-Guy Lavigueur and William Murphy

FRENCH AND ENGLISH CANADA

FACTS:

1. Sixty-three percent of Canadians have English as their mother tongue, 24% have French as their first language, and 15% have a mother tongue other than English or French.

2. More people have English as their mother tongue and fewer people have French as their native language than 10 years ago.

3. There are now fewer people with English as their mother tongue in Quebec. There are more with French as a mother tongue.

4. Bilingualism is up across the country. More than 4 000 000 Canadians can speak well enough to have a conversation in both official languages.

5. More than half of all bilingual Canadians live in Quebec. Fifty-four percent of English Quebeckers and 33% of French Quebeckers are bilingual.

6. The second most bilingual province is New Brunswick, where 30% of the population can speak both languages.

7. Young Canadians are more likely to be bilingual.

8. Eighty-five percent of Canadians studied both languages in school.

9. Ten percent of English Grade 1 students are studying in French Immersion programs where all subjects are taught in French.

10. Sixty-three percent of Canadians think bilingualism in Canada is not working. Twenty-two percent think it is a success; 15% don't know.

11. Forty-two percent of Quebeckers want to separate from Canada. Forty-two percent are against separation. Sixteen percent aren't sure.

12. Twenty-seven percent of Canadians are for separation; 59% are against it.

Instructor's Manual
Pre-reading activity and discussion

LISTENING TO CANADIANS

Before you listen: Discuss the meaning of these words:

identity	behavioral differences	advertising
impulsive	economically	logical
breakup	communicate	marvellous

Listen and write short answers.

Name: From: Age:	Douglas Black Toronto, Ont. 27 years old	Michel Gauthier Montreal, Que. 44 years old	Ruth Daley Montreal, Que. 48 years old
1. What is the difference between French and English Canadian culture?			
2. Should all Canadians become bilingual?			
3. Should Quebec separate from Canada?			

*Instructor's Manual
Tapescript and discussion

SPEAKING TO CANADIANS

Ask a Canadian about French and English Canadian culture. Discuss the answers with the class. But first, ask your instructor!

YOUR INSTRUCTOR'S ANSWERS

1. What are some of the differences between French and English Canadian culture?

___

___

___

2. Should all Canadians become bilingual? Why or why not?

___

___

___

3. Should Quebec separate from Canada? Explain your answer.

___

___

___

A CANADIAN'S ANSWERS

1. What are some of the differences between French and English Canadian culture?

___

___

___

2. Should all Canadians become bilingual? Why or why not?

___

___

___

3. Should Quebec separate from Canada? Explain your answer.

___

___

___

HONESTY PAYS

First Listening: William is waiting for a newspaper reporter who is coming over to interview him. Listen to their conversation and put the pictures in order.

Tell the story.

*Read it in *Amazing! Canadian Newspaper Stories.*
Tapescript in *Instructor's Manual*

CORRECT THE REPORTER'S NOTES

Second Listening: Correct the reporter's notes. Mark an "x" beside anything that is wrong. Then listen again to correct the mistakes.

1. ☐ *William lives in a big place.*
2. ☐ *He had $56 000 in the bank.*
3. ☐ *He found the wallet on Saturday morning.*
4. ☐ *Inside were six dollars, ID, and eighteen lottery tickets.*
5. ☐ *He kept the wallet.*
6. ☐ *He kept the tickets because he felt lucky.*
7. ☐ *A couple of days later he was watching TV and found out he had the winning ticket.*
8. ☐ *He won $9.6 million.*
9. ☐ *He was so surprised he thought he was going to have a heart attack.*
10. ☐ *He couldn't sleep at night.*
11. ☐ *He decided to return the ticket.*
12. ☐ *The owner's name and address were on the back of the tickets.*
13. ☐ *When he first tried to return the ticket, a young kid who didn't understand English slammed the door in his face.*
14. ☐ *The next night, he stayed home.*
15. ☐ *When Jean-Guy answered the door, William told him he was returning a winning lottery ticket and it was worth $7.6 million.*
16. ☐ *Jean-Guy was so happy, he gave William a $1.2 million reward.*
17. ☐ *William plans to open a night club in Montreal with the money.*

Extra: Use the corrected notes to write a newspaper article about the story.

ADJECTIVES

WITH A GROUP Think of adjectives to describe the three people in the story.

William	Jean-Guy	Yves
______________	______________	______________
______________	______________	______________
______________	______________	______________
______________	______________	______________
______________	______________	______________

Tell the class why you wrote each adjective.

Change groups and brainstorm other adjectives to describe people. Write the meaning beside each adjective.

______________: ______________________________

______________: ______________________________

______________: ______________________________

______________: ______________________________

______________: ______________________________

______________: ______________________________

______________: ______________________________

______________: ______________________________

______________: ______________________________

______________: ______________________________

Write six adjectives that describe yourself.

______________ ______________ ______________

______________ ______________ ______________

SPEAKING WITH A PARTNER Pair up and ask the following questions.

1a. Why do you think you are ______________?

1b. What makes you say you are ______________?

2. Does being ______________ run in your family ?

3. Tell me about a time when you were ______________.

4. Do you like being ______________? Why or why not?

5. Have you always been ______________?

EXPRESSING SURPRISE

First Listening: Who is surprised? Why?

CONVERSATION 1. Who: ______________________________

Why: ______________________________

CONVERSATION 2. Who: ______________________________

Why: ______________________________

CONVERSATION 3. Who: ______________________________

Why: ______________________________

Second Listening: Write the number of the conversation beside the words for expressing surprise.

☐ I don't believe it!

☐ Are you joking or what?

☐ I don't know what to say!

☐ You've got to be kidding!

☐ But it can't be!

☐ Are you sure?

☐ That's unbelievable!

☐ This is fantastic!

☐ Wow!

☐ You're joking!

☐ This is incredible!

☐ Oh my God!

☐ Are you serious?

☐ Amazing!

SPEAKING—VIDEO ROLE PLAY

Work with a partner to practice the same three conversations you heard on the tape. Write what each conversation is about in the spaces below.

1. ______________________________
2. ______________________________
3. ______________________________

Use the expressions above to show surprise.
Videotape and replay for the class. Correct any errors.

Canadian Culture

LOTTERIES

FACTS:

1. Lotteries became legal in Canada in 1968.
2. Lotto 6/49, the largest lottery, began in 1982.
3. Almost every Canadian has bought tickets at least once.
4. Canadians spend more than three billion dollars on government lotteries every year.
5. Seventy percent of Canadians buy tickets regularly.
6. Families spend about $146 a year on lotteries.
7. Quebeckers buy more tickets than other Canadians. They spend an average of $187 a year on lotto tickets.
8. Usually, the larger a family's income, the more tickets they buy. Eighty-one percent of families with an income around $50-60 000 a year spend an average of $238 a year on tickets. Forty-nine percent of families with incomes of less than $10 000 spend only $49 a year on tickets.
9. Men and women buy the same number of tickets.
10. Younger people buy more tickets.
11. Tickets cost anywhere between $0.50 and $10.
12. Prizes range from a free ticket to millions of dollars.
13. Odds of winning are from 1 in 3 to 1 in 14 000 000 000.
14. Chances of winning $100 000 or more are 1 in 500 000.
15. What did big winners do with their millions?
    78% continued buying tickets
    73% put some of the money in the bank
    44% shared the money with family
    26% did some travelling
    23% bought a new car
    15% paid off the mortgage on their house
    7% invested in bonds
    6% bought a house

16. What happens to the money Lotto 6/49 gets from ticket sales? — Almost half is returned to players as prizes.
   - Six percent goes to store owners.
   - Three percent goes to the federal government.
   - The rest is used to help out with a number of activities in different provinces—sports and recreation, cultural events, citizenship, health care, medical and scientific research, education and charitable organizations.

Instructor's Manual
Pre-reading activity and discussion

SPEAKING TO CANADIANS

Ask two Canadians the following questions and share your answers with the class.

CONVERSATION 1

1. Do you buy lottery tickets? What kind? How often?

____

2. Did you ever win any money? When? How much?

____

3. What would you do if you won the jackpot?

____

____

CONVERSATION 2

1. Do you buy lottery tickets? What kind? How often?

____

2. Did you ever win any money? When? How much?

____

3. What would you do if you won the jackpot?

____

____

CHAPTER 13: LIFE ON OTHER PLANETS

Donna Cooper, St. John's, Nfld.

Joel Simkin, Winnipeg, Man.

LIFE ON OTHER PLANETS

FACTS:

1. On October 3, 1843, Charles Cooper of Sarnia, Ontario, saw three men, perfectly white, sailing through the air.

2. In the spring of 1941, Arthur Matthews of Quebec City, Quebec, met with two beings from Venus. They were around six feet tall, had bright blue eyes and golden hair.

3. On May 12, 1958, Frederick Dally from Kitchener, Ontario, saw a 7-metre, saucer-shaped UFO over a neighbour's house. It didn't move or make any noise. That same day, another person reported seeing the same UFO.

4. In the spring of 1959, Mrs. E. Walker from Abbotsford, B.C., saw what she thought was a large star. Then it began to change colour—blue, green, red, white. It bounced up and down a few times and moved in a triangular shape. It kept changing colours while moving.

5. On May 20, 1967, Stephen Michalak, a Polish Canadian from Winnipeg, Manitoba, went looking for gold at Falcon Lake. There he saw two red, glowing, cigar-shaped objects in the sky. One stayed only for about three minutes and the other landed 50 metres away on a flat rock. It didn't make a sound but the colour changed from red to orange. The rock changed colour as well. It went from red to red-grey to light grey. A purple light shone down from the top of the ship and hurt Stephen's eyes when he looked at it.

   As he moved closer to the craft, he heard voices. At first, he thought it was a U.S. ship so he called out in English—no answer. Then he tried Russian—no response. He tried German, Italian, French and Ukrainian—still no answer. Stephen spoke in English once again and moved even closer to the ship. He stuck his head inside the door and saw lights shining in every direction. He noticed the walls were half a metre thick and hot to touch. He burned the glove he was wearing.

   Suddenly the craft moved to the left and he felt a pain in his chest. One of the lights hit him and he fell to the ground. Stephen was badly burned. When he looked back the ship was rising above the treetops and began to change colour. Within seconds, it was gone.

6. In 1971, John Grosskurth from Medicine Hat, Alberta, saw a 30-metre cigar-shaped object travelling about 15 metres above the road. There was a large white light shining from the front.

7. In November 1974, Stan Mickus saw a white light and it headed straight for him. Later he noticed he had deep cuts, scars, and even a hole in his right leg.

   Under hypnosis, he found out two beings had kidnapped him, taken him aboard their ship, performed medical tests, and had taken skin and bone samples.

8. In 1974, Nancy DuPlessis-Merrill saw a huge light shining on some trees near her house near Scotch Lake, New Brunswick. She lived in the country and there were no other neighbours nearby.

   Later, she and her husband saw the light following their car. Sometimes, it shone into the bathroom window.

   In 1982, she was lying on the couch and her dog ran upstairs and hid under the bed. She looked outside and saw a huge oval-shaped space ship.

9. In 1987 Ronald Marcel of Vancouver saw a UFO at Lion's Bay. He noticed a jet flying across the sky. The UFO passed over it and was going five times faster. It must have been going 3000 miles an hour.

10. On February 20, 1992, Monika MacKenzie of Kamloops, B.C. was walking to work at 6:30 a.m. when she saw a red and blue ball-shaped object zipping toward the ground.

    The same day, Al Hepworth, an airport worker, reported seeing a bright blue ball flying 1000 metres overhead while he was driving to work.

Instructor's Manual
Pre-reading activity and discussion.
Alternate activity: Have students make questions about the facts and ask them to a partner.

LISTENING TO CANADIANS — Interview 1

Before You Listen: 1. Discuss the meaning of these words:

it blew me away | zoomed | communicate | curiosity

2. Read the statements below. Ask about any words you don't know.

Listen and tick off [✔] all correct statements. Mark an "x" beside those that are wrong. Correct the mistakes.

1. ☐ Donna saw a UFO when she was around twelve years old.
2. ☐ She thinks there is life on other planets because there are too many people spotting and seeing things for it all to be stories or made up.
3. ☐ She saw a flying saucer late at night.
4. ☐ It was egg-shaped and had flashing lights.
5. ☐ It was on the ground, beside her house for two hours.
6. ☐ Donna thinks she saw two extra-terrestrials in the UFO.
7. ☐ She believes some people who say they've seen UFO's, but she doesn't believe all of them.
8. ☐ She thinks extra-terrestrials have visited Earth.
9. ☐ She thinks they are tall and hairy.
10. ☐ Donna believes they are very intelligent and can understand any language, even English!
11. ☐ She thinks they would come to Earth to take back people to their planet.
12. ☐ She thinks Canada should start a space exploration program.

Donna Cooper, 29, St. John's, Nfld.

**Instructor's Manual*
Tapescript and discussion

LISTENING TO CANADIANS — Interview 2

Before You Listen: 1. Discuss the meaning of these words:

universe	Mars/Venus/planets	doubt	invisible
non-verbal	brain-to-brain contact	humans	waste of money

2. What questions will the interviewer ask?

1. Life on other planets: ______________________________

____

____

____

____

____

2. Seen UFO: ______________________________
3. Seen extra-terrestrial: ______________________________
4. Believe other people: ______________________________

Joel Simkin, 45, Winnipeg, Man.

____

____

____

5. Extra-terrestrials visited Earth: ______________________________
6. Looks: ______________________________
7. How communicate: ______________________________
8. Intelligent: ______________________________
9. Why visit Earth: ______________________________

____

10. Space exploration program for Canada: ______________________________

____

**Instructor's Manual*
Tapescript and discussion

SPEAKING — LIFE ON OTHER PLANETS

Write the questions you heard the interviewer ask in the boxes on the left. Then ask them of two students from different countries.

Name:		
1.		
2.		
3.		
4.		
5.		
6.		
7.		
8.		
9.		
10.		

VISITORS FROM ABOVE

First Listening: Dorothy is a guest on a call-in radio talk show. People call in with their questions and comments. Listen to the interview and put the pictures in order.

Tell the story.

*Read it in *Amazing! Canadian Newspaper Stories.*
Tapescript in *Instructor's Manual*

CALLERS NUMBER 1, 2 & 3

Second Listening: Listen to the callers again and fill in the information below.

CALLER 1

Name: ______________________________

From: ______________________________

Question 1: ______________________________

Question 2: ______________________________

Question 3: ______________________________

Question 4: ______________________________

CALLER 2

Name: ______________________________

From: ______________________________

Opinion: ______________________________

____

CALLER 3

Name: ______________________________

From: ______________________________

Question 1: ______________________________

Question 2: ______________________________

Question 3: ______________________________

Question 4: ______________________________

SPEAKING — RADIO TALK SHOWS

1. Work in groups of five and role play the radio talk show. One person is the announcer and introduces Dorothy, tells where she lives and about her job. Then the announcer accepts calls from callers #1, 2 and 3.

2. Have another radio talk show about UFOs. The instructor is the announcer and students can call in with their opinions.

3. Students work in groups to think of other topics for radio talk shows and suggest them to the group at large.

DESCRIBING

Four people describe UFOs or extra-terrestrials they have seen. Write the number of the monologue beside the illustration it describes.

What words do people use to describe UFOs and extra-terrestrials?

SPEAKING — DESCRIBING AN EXTRA-TERRESTRIAL

This is a picture of an extra-terrestrial. Describe it to your partner who will draw it. Draw the UFO she/he describes.

Describe this illustration.

Draw in this space.

SPEAKING — DESCRIBING A UFO

Your partner will describe an extra-terrestrial. Draw it below. Next, describe the UFO and ask your partner to draw it.

Draw in this space.	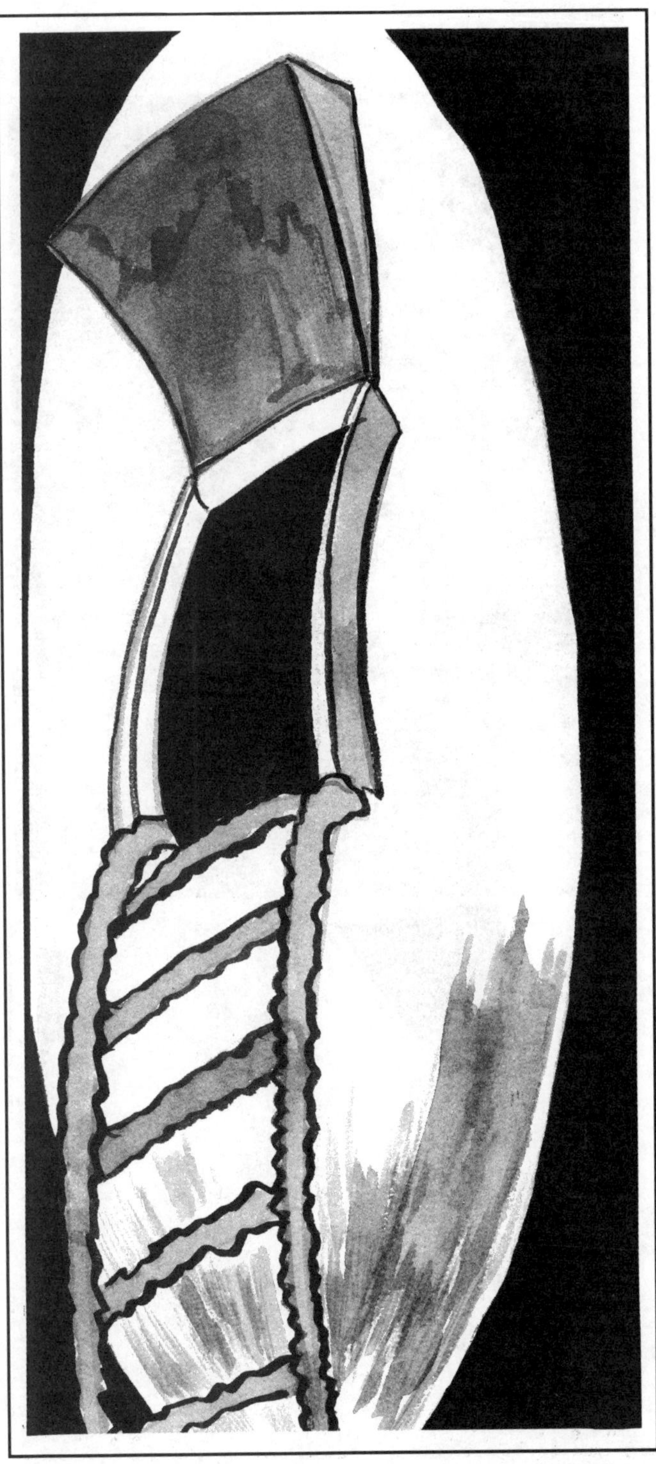 Describe this illustration.

CHAPTER 14: PEOPLE WITH DISABILITIES

Sandra Meredith, Edmonton, Alta.

Archie Havard, Edmonton, Alta.

PEOPLE WITH DISABILITIES

FACTS:

1. Over three and a half million, or one in eight Canadians, have some kind of disability.
2. Of those with a disability, 66% have a mobility disability—they cannot walk, move from room to room, or stand for a long time.
3. Fifty-eight percent have an agility disability—they have difficulty bending, reaching, dressing, getting in and out of bed and grasping with their hands.
4. Thirty-two percent have a hearing disability.
5. Eighteen percent have a visual disability.
6. Eight percent have difficulty speaking.
7. Sixty-four percent have two or more disabilities. Thirty-three percent have three or more.
8. More people become disabled as they get older. For example,
   5% of 0-14 year olds are disabled,
   6% of 15-34 year olds are disabled,
   16% of 35-64 year olds are disabled,
   46% of people over 65 are disabled, and
   82% of people over 85 are disabled.
9. There are more disabled males from 0-55 years of age, but after 55 there are more disabled women.
10. Forty-eight percent of disabled persons are in the labour force. Seventy-eight percent of the non-disabled population are working or on UIC.
11. Eight percent of the disabled live in institutions or homes for seniors. Over three quarters of those in institutions are 65 years of age or older.
12. Eighty-nine percent of disabled persons often participate in activities outside their homes.
13. Thirty-one percent participate in a sport three times a week.
14. Most people with disabilities are married but more are single than those without disabilities.
15. Twenty-two percent of disabled adults aged 15-64 use wheelchairs.

**Instructor's Manual*
Pre-reading activity and discussion

LISTENING TO CANADIANS — Interview 1

Before You Listen

A. You will hear three Canadians answer the following questions. What do you think they will say?

1. What disabilities do you know about?

2. How do you think life is different for someone with a disability?

3. Do you think Canada does enough for people with disabilites?

4. How does Canada compare to other countries in its treatment of people with disabilities?

5. What do you know about Rick Hansen?

B. Discuss the meaning of these words:

raised funds   minority   rights

C. Read the statements below. Ask about any words you don't know.

Listen and tick off [✔] all correct statements. Mark an "x" beside those that are wrong. Correct the mistakes.

1. ☐ Anne says people with disabilities are those who can't do what other people do because the world is not made for people like them.

2. ☐ She says disabled people have more freedom.

3. ☐ Jocylyn Lovell, a gold medal cyclist, was her friend.

4. ☐ He got hit by a car and now he's paralysed.

5. ☐ Jocylyn didn't need much money to live.

6. ☐ He needed to have a house built to his needs.

7. ☐ He needed some special equipment to brush his teeth.

8. ☐ Anne took part in a cycling trip to raise money for him.

9. ☐ They raised $100 000 for a house and a truck.

Sandra Meredith, 29, Edmonton, Alta.

10. ☐ Anne doesn't think Canada does enough for people with disabilities.

11. ☐ She thinks companies could do more to help people with disabilities.

12. ☐ Her husband works at a lab and he told her the lab benches were too high, so short people could not work there.

13. ☐ She works at the airport and she thinks they should make larger seats in airplanes because someone weighing over 300 pounds could not fit in the seats they have now.

14. ☐ She said Rick Hansen wheeled around Canada.

15. ☐ He talked about the rights of disabled people to raise awareness.

16. ☐ Rick's trip was important to Anne because she learned that disabled people could do a lot if they were willing to help themselves.

Rick Hansen: "I want to wheel around the world."

Instructor's Manual
Tapescript and discussion

LISTENING TO CANADIANS — Interview 2

Before You Listen: Discuss the meaning of these words:

MS
self-conscious
facilities
paraplegic
ramps
freaks
quadriplegic
Prairies
social programs

Listen and fill in the missing information.

1. Disabilities: ______________________________

____

____

____

____

____

2. How life is different: ______________________________

____

____

____

____

____

____

Archie Havard, 55, Edmonton, Alta.

3. Canada do enough: ______________________________

____

____

____

____

____

____

4. Other countries: ______________________________

____

____

____

5. Rick Hansen: ______________________________

____

____

LISTENING TO CANADIANS — Interview 3

Before You Listen: Discuss the meaning of these words:

cerebral palsy	multiple sclerosis	uncomfortable	fit in
accept	Third World	outcast	for instance

Listen and fill in the missing information.

1. Disabilities: ______________________________

____

____

____

____

____

Anne Letourneau, 32, Montreal, Que.

2. How life is different: ______________________________

____

____

____

____

____

____

3. Canada do enough: ______________________________

____

____

____

____

4. Other countries: ______________________________

____

____

____

____

5. Rick Hansen: ______________________________

____

*Instructor's Manual
Tapescript and discussion

RICK HANSEN: A CANADIAN HERO

First Listening: A boy asks his father to tell him about Rick Hansen. Listen to their conversation and put the pictures in order.

Tell the story.

*Read it in *Amazing! Canadian Newspaper Stories.*
Tapescript in *Instructor's Manual*

LISTENING FOR FACTS

Second Listening: You are the son. Listen again and take notes for school.

- Accident when ________[1] years old in 19 ________[2] while coming home from a ________[3] trip
- Truck turned over, Rick __________[4] his __________[5]
- Hospital, found out he was ____________________[6]
- A year later, ____[7]
- He wanted to ________________________[8] and raise money for ____________________[9]and ____________________[10]
- Went to school and got degree in ________________[11] Education at __________[12]
- Won world championships in __________________[13] and ______________[14]
- Started world tour in March of 19 __________[15]
- Not many __________[16] came
- Roof rack ________________[17] truck
- Wheeled over __________[18] mountain ranges and through __________[19] continents
- Problems: ________________[20], ________________[21], ______________[22]
- Robbed __________[23] times
- __________[24] flat tires
- Wheeled up the ________________[25] China
- Raised ______________[26] during tour
- ______________[27] people greeted him at the finish line
- Rick Hansen is ________________________________[28]

Reacting to the Story—Intercultural Awareness

SPEAKING — HEROES AND FAMOUS PEOPLE

A hero is a brave person who did something great. A famous person is well-known because of something they have done. Ask students about heroes and famous people in their countries.

Who do you think of as a hero or famous person in your country? Why?

1. Name: ________________ Answer: ____

____

2. Name: ________________ Answer: ____

____

3. Name: ________________ Answer: ____

____

4. Name: ________________ Answer: ____

____

CONGRATULATING

Listen to the people at Rick Hansen's "Welcome Home Party" and tick off [✔] the expressions you hear for congratulating.

1. ☐ You're my kind of guy!
2. ☐ Congratulations!
3. ☐ Congratulations on...
4. ☐ We're proud of you!
5. ☐ Fantastic!
6. ☐ Excellent!
7. ☐ You're #1!
8. ☐ What a guy!
9. ☐ Way to go!
10. ☐ Good for you!
11. ☐ Good show!
12. ☐ You did it!
13. ☐ Wonderful!
14. ☐ Great stuff!
15. ☐ You're a winner!

Speaking — CONGRATULATING

Do you know any other ways to express congratulations? Discuss which expressions would be appropriate in the following situations.

1. Your sister just had a baby.
2. A co-worker just got engaged.
3. Your son was accepted at university.
4. Your neighbour graduated from university.
5. A classmate did very well in an English test.
6. Your bank manager lost eighty pounds.
7. Your doctor just quit smoking.
8. Your best friend finally got a job.
9. Your daughter got a fantastic report card at school.
10. Your boss just got a promotion.

Practice each conversation with a different partner. Use the expressions above.